History on our Side

Wales and the 1984–85 Miners' Strike

Hywel Francis

ICONAU

Published by Iconau
Fernbank
Ferryside
SA17 5SR

ISBN: 978 1905762 45 3

First published in 2009
© Hywel Francis
All rights reserved

Design & typesetting: Lucy Llewellyn

Cover montage: Hazel Gillings & Gary Bevan, Tondu Photo Workshop
Back cover image: South Wales Coalfield Archive
Author photo: Peter Knowles LMPA

Printed and bound by Dinefwr Press, Llandybïe, Wales

British Library Cataloguing in Publication Data

A catalogue record of this book is available from the British Library.

For

David, Evan, Elis, Elena and Aled

So that they will remember their roots in the
coalfields of Derbyshire and South Wales

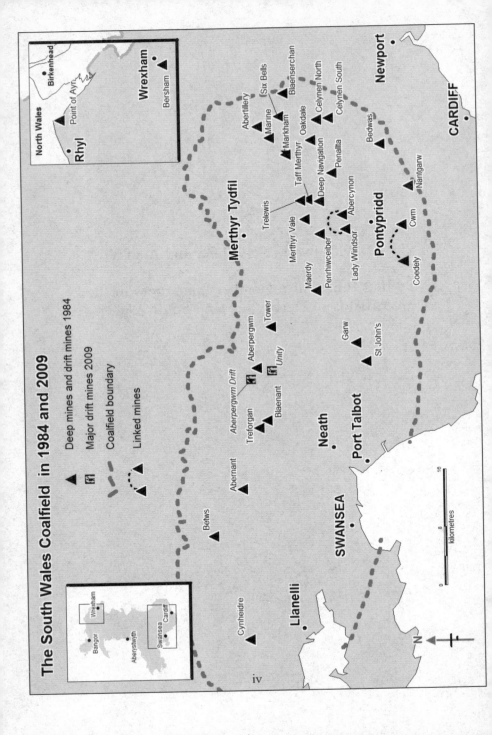

The South Wales Coalfield in 1984 and 2009

Contents

Foreword

The great miners' strike of 1984–85 was a monumental and momentous industrial and political struggle. It was a battle for a sane and balanced energy policy based on indigenous British coal and for the long-term sustainability of working-class communities in Wales and throughout Britain. It was a long and courageous strike, and I am proud to say Welsh miners, including my own Tower miners, played a leading role.

The solidarity within our communities, across Wales and across the world was without precedent, and we could not have lasted for long without it. The greatest solidarity of all was from the women of the coalfields, not just supporting, but leading the miners alongside us.

My friend and comrade Hywel Francis has told this story with both passion and objectivity. He is well qualified to do so, rooted as he is in the South Wales valleys, the son of one of the most distinguished Welsh miners' leaders, Dai Francis. Hywel has remarkable credentials as an historian of the miners and as a leading adult educator in valley communities as the founder of the Community University of the Valleys and the South Wales Miners' Library.

But he and his wife Mair were also active participants in the events which he faithfully records, as he was both chair of his local miners' support group and the pathbreaking Wales Congress in Support of Mining Communities.

The title of this study, *History on our Side*, derived as it is from my fellow Tower miner, Robert True, is testimony to the validity of our struggle. Coal is returning, and our valleys' communities, despite the deprivation which followed on the strike, continue to embrace collectivist and democratic values. I cannot put my hand on my heart and say that Hywel and I totally agree on all his conclusions, but Hywel and I have had many argumentative but wonderfully enjoyable hours debating not only the 1984–85 miners' strike but all the strikes and all important issues of our time.

This is an important book about a necessary struggle in which so many of us were proud to take part. As with all experiences of this kind, we must learn the lessons of our proud past.

Tyrone O'Sullivan
Chairman, Tower Colliery Ltd
(the only workers' owned coal mine in the world)

Introduction:

A Personal Testimony

In the early autumn of 2008 I decided to bring together my earlier writings and my still strong memories to publish a twenty-fifth anniversary history of the miners' strike in Wales. The title comes from the words and actions of 1984–85 and what was happening around me in my Aberavon constituency, and across the world, in 2008.

This is not by any means an academic study although it does have some characteristics of my earlier life as an historian. It is more the attempt of a political activist to make sense of the crisis then engulfing the community in which my family for at least five generations had lived and worked.

As a labour historian and oral historian, I was very aware from the early days of the strike that we were living in momentous and historic times and in a small way I was part of the unfolding events. I started to keep a diary but we all became aware of police surveillance and I went through a gradual process of self-censorship. My friends Phil Thomas and Penny Smith of the Welsh Council for Civil and Political

Liberties recorded miners' experiences for their book *Striking Back* but they hid their tapes under floorboards. We were conscious too of phone tapping as police monitored picket movements. Tupperware parties and swimming in the Afan Lido were code for occupations of Cynheidre colliery, as revealed in John Morgans' recently published diaries, *Journey of a Lifetime* (2008).

In June 1984 I noted in my diary an event which was to anticipate the coming community mobilisation:

6 June D. Day + 40. My birthday. Drop off Mair at Pontrhydyfen [Primary School] on a cold clear summer morning. Drive up the Afan Valley. As I get to Cynonville – white painted slogan on a bus shelter, 'Save Our Buses'. Within minutes an army of people coming towards me on the road – quite a sight on an empty road. The people of Blaengwynfi on the march to Cymmer? 'Who are you taking pictures for?' 'The Miners' Library in Swansea.' 'Oh that's all right.' 'Have you seen any police on your travels?' said the leader – a woman. 'No' says I. Led by a phalanx of women. Then behind the younger kids. At rear teenage girls smoking. Followed by the only 2 men – straggling behind. Smaller groups further back.

Moments before Mair and I were discussing the same problem in our valley.

I recently spoke to my constituents in the former mining communities of Abergwynfi, Blaengwynfi, Croeserw and Duffryn Rhondda in the Afan Valley of how I was reminded of 1984–85 by their current community campaigning as illustrated by my diaries for the period. The global banking crisis and the Labour Government's response in reverting to the old socialist values of public ownership was again an echo of what the 1980s was all about. And as if to further underline parallels with the past, I have recently been having talks with unions and management about the sinking in my constituency of the Margam New Mine, an abandoned project from two decades ago.

The title then comes from all this and from the words of a Tower striking miner in June 1984, Robert True of Treherbert, who said to me, 'Surely, we can't lose, history is on our side!' Sadly it would take more than history to achieve victory although it played a big part in the resistance.

Looking back now, a quarter of a century later, those twelve months represent a personal and political watershed for so many. I reflect on my own life at the time, a university tutor in adult education, teaching on miners' day release courses and in valley communities, living in a village, Crynant, with two working collieries employing nearly one thousand miners.

I had visited the Appalachian coalfields with six rank-and-file miners from Brynlliw and Maerdy in May 1979, just at the very moment that Margaret Thatcher won her momentous General Election victory. Our report, *South Wales Miners in America*, mirrored our own past and what was to be our own future – hostile employers, non-unionism, scab unionism, anti-union laws and expanding opencast mining.

I was supportive of the battles over Deep Dyffryn in 1979 and the short strikes in 1981 and 1983, both of which were mere skirmishes in comparison with what was about to engulf us.

On St David's Day, 1st March 1984, my book *Miners Against Fascism* was launched at the South Wales Miners' Library in the presence of miners' leaders, politicians and academics; no one expected that within less than two weeks the British coalfields would have lurched into the biggest industrial struggle since 1926. Very soon I became totally immersed in the strike, visiting Scotland in early April, where after giving a lecture at the university on Arthur Horner, I met with my father's old friend, the National Union of Mineworkers (NUM) vice president Michael McGahey, who took me to meet David Hamilton, a strike leader at Monktonhall Colliery who later became a valued Parliamentary colleague and a chair of the All Party Parliamentary Coalfields Community Group. We were both then active members of the Communist Party.

A short time later I visited the Leicestershire and South Derbyshire coalfields to assist the South Wales pickets, led by Peter Evans of Merthyr Vale, in bringing together the small numbers of strikers who eventually called themselves 'The Dirty Thirty', and whose leaders were Mick (Rico) Richmond and Malcolm (Benny) Pinnegar. While in Leicestershire there was an attempted breakaway at Cynheidre in West Wales and I returned with the 'Dirty Thirty' leaders to help organise the local demonstration.

One of my diary entries from 22nd May when I was in Bagworth, Leicestershire, said chillingly,

Police Inspector walks up to Eddie's house as we arrive. Looks up drive and then walks slowly back. Talk about harassment.

And this following phone call to Tony Ciano in Cynheidre:

His family have had anonymous phone calls. Threats of blowing up his home. Slept elsewhere last night.

And later, summing up the situation,

Massive police presence. Two buses at Bagworth pit with sleeping facilities in two large marquees nearby.

On 7th June I participated in the NUM mass lobby of Parliament. Nearly two decades later I recalled the occasion in my maiden speech because it was the exact anniversary of the return of the Labour Government and my first election in 2001:

> The date 7th June was the day in 1984 when I was outside the House with tens of thousands of people from mining communities all over Britain.... For many Labour Members, there is a certain poetic justice about the date of 7th June.

My diary entry of the day revealed the tensions and solidarity of the time (and lack of it):

> V. good public response – went down Fleet St. Arrived at Jubilee Gardens. Fracas. Snatch squads. Charge led by Kent Miners' Wives. Police Inspector on Westminster Bridge said 'we cannot cope'. In minutes police on horseback arrive. Saw soldier driving police van. Got caught in another fracas at the outside of the lobby. Lot of anger. Took lot of pix. One miner said to a black policeman – 'there's no black in the Union Jack'.

I remember thinking at the time, 'If there's a fight here, I will be on the side of the policeman.' For me those words were shocking and thankfully untypical.

Our local support group which I chaired was well established by June 1984 and over the summer I spent time planning the NUM's National Eisteddfod presence at Lampeter with Labour member Deian Hopkin along with Rhodri Williams and Wynfford James, two former leaders of the Welsh Language Society. The links we made at the Eisteddfod prepared the way for the Wales Congress in Support of Mining Communities in October. At the time of the Eisteddfod our support group bank accounts were sequestrated, illegally, and with the legal help of law lecturer Phil Thomas of Cardiff University we successfully freed our funds and stashed them away with sympathetic local shopkeepers who supplied food for families for the rest of the strike.

Later in August I was in Moscow researching newly opened archives for a biography of Arthur Horner, the miners' leader. With letters of introduction from area president Emlyn Williams and national president Arthur Scargill, I met with Soviet miners' leader Michael Srebny who arranged for me to visit the Donbas coalfield in the Ukraine, which my father had visited in 1952. I witnessed major collections of money for striking British miners at the pitheads and was told that these funds were unlikely to reach us because of diplomatic difficulties. On my return I told the NUM about these collections, and I assume those funds did eventually reach the NUM via the French trade unions and the International Transport Workers' Federation.

Throughout this period I was working closely with my friend Kim Howells who was emerging as a major figure in the NUM in South Wales as its main press spokesman.

We organised with Huw Beynon of Durham University and Bob Fryer of Northern College a series of conferences for striking miners and women support groups from several coalfields to make some sense of the wider political and economic contexts of the strike.

It was in a discussion with Kim and separately with Wynfford James, Menna Elfyn and Ffred Francis and also with Rev John Morgans, Moderator of the United Reform Church in

Wales, that we came on the need to create an all-Wales organisation to mobilise politically and financially on a more systematic basis. The Wales Congress in Support of Mining Communities was the result, and one of its highlights was a launching conference in Cardiff and later a big concert at Treorchy with the Flying Pickets and the writer Molly Parkin, who was originally from Pontycymmer.

Hardship increased with winter coming upon us. The shock of the taxi driver's death in November and the euphoria of Christmas solidarity ebbing away in the New Year meant we were living in difficult times. I became increasingly anxious that a dramatic collapse was likely if a compromise agreement could not be secured. I remember on a bitterly cold day in December after I gave the funeral oration to miners' leader Will Paynter a worried Michael McGahey told me 'we live in dangerous times'. Kim thought my statement in praising Paynter's qualities of leadership and hatred of the 'cult of the personality' was an attack on Arthur Scargill.

Even in the last few weeks of the strike the resolve in South Wales still remained strong and I was particularly aware of this as I was asked by the NUM to help distribute funds to pickets across the coalfield. I was also impressed by the determination of the women's support groups and assisted in getting groups to occupy Cynheidre Colliery: one woman was too busy to go because she had promised to go poaching with her father.

My visits, however, that winter to Nottingham, Yorkshire and Durham revealed to me that the strike was not 'solid' and confirmed the television reports of a collapsing struggle.

Such visits convinced me too that there was a political paralysis at national level, locked in as it was to a 'no surrender' strategy. I believed the only way an orderly return could be achieved would be through the strongest coalfield –

South Wales – taking the lead at a national conference. And that too was difficult to bring about because of the determination of so many of our communities who refused to believe that the strike was collapsing in other coalfields.

As the strike ground on, I wondered more and more about those who were breaking the strike, particularly as so many of them were in other coalfields and some of whose representatives wanted the strike to continue 'to the last drop of South Wales blood'. I began to believe too that the slogan 'a scab is a scab forever' was strategically illogical and unsustainable. South Wales pickets came back from Nottinghamshire warning of a 'scab solidarity' and of the ineffectiveness of mass picketing.

When the trickle back to work eventually came to South Wales, my personal views changed irrevocably. Dai Smith and I had written of such crises, at a distance, in *The Fed*. But then I could see such situations at first hand. I was asked by NUM lodge officials, by local police and by one colliery manager to speak to two miners who had broken with the strike. I was asked to intervene because of the potential dire consequences locally. I think my intervention brought them back 'towards us', at least for the moment. They were frightened, isolated human beings, manipulated by darker and wider Government forces. They reminded me of the lines from Idris Davies' epic poem of 1926, *Gwalia Deserta* (1938):

... The great dream and the swift disaster,
The fanatic and the traitor, and more than all,
The bravery of the simple, faithful folk?

'The traitors' were the ones caught in between – they were not the 'super scabs' who organised the return. And what of those who bayed for blood and at the same time, rumour had it, plotted in their beer their own return to work (was it in the 'Old Swan' or was it in the 'New Swan'?) or who hobbled all through the strike? What price their 'solidarity'?

My most vivid memories of that terrible and glorious year of 1984–85 are to do with the courage of the people of our local mining communities particularly in the latter stages of the struggle, and also Dean Hancock and Russell Shankland who were imprisoned as a consequence of the taxi driver's death: I corresponded with them and helped develop some of their educational programmes over a number of years.

In my own mining locality I believed then that our support group was the best in Britain. It was the best because we were blessed with talented and committed people who rose to the challenge of developing what became an alternative welfare state. Kay Bowen of Dyffryn Cellwen was our remarkable food co-ordinator who saw to it that our ten food distribution centres sustained more than a thousand families for twelve months.

This could not have been done without fund-raising. One of our principal fundraisers was Dai Donovan of Ynyswen, later a full-time officer of the broadcasting union, BECTU. He built strong links in London with print unions, Brent NALGO, a range of political organisations, and the gay and lesbian community (who donated a new minibus). Arguably the most successful fundraiser was the secretary of Onllwyn Miners' Welfare Club, Alun (Ali) Thomas, later the deputy leader of Neath Port Talbot County Borough Council. He was away so much, mainly in Ireland and North Wales, that he became known as 'our roving ambassador' and 'our foreign secretary'. His Irish connection has been sustained by my friend Francis Devine of the union SIPTU, who played an outstanding role in building cultural and political links between the Dulais Valley and Ireland.

These fundraisers were responsible for major concerts. They involved the South Wales Striking Miners' Choir that was created out of the many local male voice choirs by Keith Bufton of Crynant and Phil Bowen, chairman of the Blaenant NUM Lodge. These concerts included such famous performers and bands as Elvis Costello, Billy Bragg, Jimmy Somerville and the Communards and the Flying Pickets. Phil also organised the Welsh Striking Miners' Rugby Team, which went on a fundraising tour of Italy.

These funds, amounting to £350,000, were looked after by our treasurer, Christine Powell of Seven Sisters, appropriately a maths teacher, and her fearsome dog Butch who slept on top of the money overnight before it was deposited in the local bank by her striking miner husband, Stuart. And to complete the family team, Christine's late father Stuart Kemeys was our enthusiastic press officer.

We were also fortunate to have the support of an older generation of retired miners, wives and widows who gave generously of their time, their experiences and their money too. There were people like Councillor Tom Jones ('Long Tom' or 'Makarios' because of his height and distinctive beard) and Edwina Roberts with her borrowed big bass drum to 'entertain' super scabs at Cynheidre.

The support group also produced its own weekly newspaper, *The Valleys' Star*, whose main editors were Frank Rees of Ystradgynlais and Margaret Donovan from Ynyswen. This was distributed to our supporters all over the world and to the striking families, in their food parcels. Although the strike resulted in much anxiety for local families, we were lucky to escape the violence which bedevilled other areas. We were fortunate that our wise picket organisers saw virtue in talking rather than fighting. At one Staffordshire pit, Phil Bowen addressed a mass meeting for so long they surrendered!

Blaenant Colliery's Lyn Harper (later a deputy-leader of Neath Port Talbot Council) and Howard Davies (later agent to the Neath MP Peter Hain) as well as Treforgan Colliery's Keith Bartlett of Banwen and the Ken Williams of Pantyffordd were always anxious to avoid conflict within our villages. For that reason, our communities were not bitterly divided after the strike.

But what made the local struggle so different was the role of women. They did not simply support; they led. Our support group secretary, Hefina Headon of Seven Sisters, was quite outstanding in her courage and political leadership, in her public speaking (including the big Afan Lido Rally), fundraising, picketing and unique style of minute taking.

In the development of a distinct women's support group, led by Sian James (later Labour MP for Swansea East) and Margaret Donovan, a group of women emerged who were able to go anywhere to speak, fundraise or picket, and even occupy Cynheidre Colliery, not once, but twice.

The centre of our local struggle was the Onllwyn Miners' Welfare Club and Hall, known far and wide in that period as 'the palace of culture'. That was where the food was distributed to the ten centres, every Friday, where the strike committee met on Sunday mornings and the support group on Sunday evenings. It was here too that we held our annual commemoration of the start of the strike. It became known as the Glorious 12th.

Hefina Headon always reminded her audiences to be proud of our struggles. She was right to be proud of struggling for our communities. Without those struggles then, I doubt if we would be here today.

In my own life and work I converted my NUM day release courses into daytime and evening classes for support groups in such places as Ystradgynlais, Onllwyn and Blaengwynfi where we tried to discuss 'objectively and historically' the big events through which we were living. One of my Swansea classes also worked with our local women's support group to produce 'Smiling and Splendid Women', a video account of the strike through their eyes.

The great fear that engulfed the South Wales valleys at the end of the strike was that the breaking up of the NUM would lead to privatisation and the virtual end of coal mining in Britain. I remember discussing the true meaning of the defeat with one of our coalfield's organic intellectuals, Allan Baker, the secretary of the Oakdale NUM Lodge. He told me to read Christopher Hill's book *The Experience of Defeat: Milton and Some Contemporaries* (1984).

One sentence at the beginning of the book described the challenge before us:

> The experience of defeat [in 1660 with the collapse of the Cromwellian Revolution] meant recognising the collapse of the system of ideas which had previously sustained action, and attempting new explanations, new perspectives. (p. 17)

History Invades the Valleys

By the summer of 1984 striking miners and their families increasingly asked, 'How long was the strike in 1926?', and increasingly too there was an irrational sense that struggles of the past somehow added up to 'we have too much history to be defeated' and 'history being on our side'. I well remember speaking at a fundraising event in Glyncorrwg in the depths of winter about the 'Cymmer riots' which were probably the worst industrial disturbances in all the British coalfields during the 1926 lockout. Despite all the best efforts to focus on a sane energy policy, history weighed heavily upon us and the slogan of 'handing mining jobs from fathers to sons' was more about looking backwards rather than forwards. 1984–85 in South Wales cannot be fully understood without some historical perspective.

The use of the state-apparatus through co-ordinated police action, a hostile press, fines and imprisonment ranged against traditional collectivist responses by the miners of mass picketing, food distribution and fundraising was so reminiscent of earlier struggles, especially 1926. The parallels between

1926 and 1984–85 were self-evident. Conducting the new struggles as if they were a re-enactment posed serious problems, but history was deep in the psyche of our communities.

The involvement of the police and the courts in industrial disputes was nothing new to the South Wales valleys. It was as old as the industry itself. A common thread is to be found throughout the long and turbulent industrial and social history of the coalfield: an alliance of employers, police, troops, informers, the press, magistrates, courts and scabs – indeed a combination of the state locally and nationally – conspires to 'keep the peace' and 'protect property' by ranging themselves against the miners, their union and their communities.

At the heart of the matter was the miners' union and its relationship to its members, its communities and, above all, to its industry. The South Wales Miners' Federation was popularly known as 'the Fed' and despite the change in name – it became the South Wales Area of the NUM – and an obvious decline in size and influence, it continued to play a vital and, for the most part, benign role. In 1917 its constitution was changed to include a pledge to abolish capitalism. This was its way of committing itself to removing all the injustices and hardships suffered by its communities over decades.

Also in 1917, and equally revealing, the Commission of Inquiry into Industrial Unrest in South Wales reported:

The hostility to capitalism has now become part of the political creed of the majority of trade unionists in the mining industry.... In mining districts 'The Federation' is ever present in the minds of the men, and although they often refer to the organisation in hard terms, their belief in it as a means of securing their economic emancipation is deep-rooted.

In all the major industrial and political struggles of the nineteenth century in South Wales, employers and magistrates (sometimes of course they were one and the same) never hesitated in calling in troops, extra police or swearing in special constables. Sometimes they did all three. Their greatest fear was the spread of the idea of struggle through what ultimately became known as 'marching gangs' – an early form of 'flying pickets'. It has to be remembered that for much of the nineteenth century many trade union activities were illegal, and only very gradually and grudgingly were industrial and democratic rights won for the miners and the working class as a whole.

The earliest form of trade unionism in the South Wales coalfield, 'the Scotch Cattle' dominated some of the early decades of the nineteenth century. By their very nature – because unions were illegal – these bands of miners relied heavily on secrecy. Warning notes and letters, attacks on company and scabs' property and midnight visits were the order of the day. They were on occasions capable of confronting and defeating regular troops. Magistrates, police and employers despaired at the elusiveness of the 'Cattle' who used these methods to instil a sense of solidarity into this newly emerging working class. Their code of conduct, 'the Scotch law', was permeated by a strong sense of natural justice. Anyone who broke ranks in a strike was ostracised in the community. The rough treatment of scabs could be interpreted as 'intimidation' but so could be the 'famine' and 'distress' imposed on communities by coal owners, ironmasters and their judicial and military allies.

Most memorable was the Chartist Rising in Newport in November 1839, the biggest political insurrection in modern British history involving armed marchers from the Gwent valleys, a confrontation with the military, at least sixteen deaths, political trials and transportation. A re-enactment of the march by Gwent miners in 1984 underlined the enduring legacy, particularly the parallels with the struggle for economic justice and political democracy.

When British miners were locked out in 1921 for refusing cuts in wages, a conference of Cabinet Ministers on 9th April, 1921, agreed that:

> ... the Admiralty should immediately form a battalion for service on land (in South Wales) from such naval ratings as were available [and] that in view of the expected arrival of troops from Silesia one battalion should be moved immediately by railway from London to Wales for the purpose of freeing the three companies at Cardiff for use in more disturbed areas.

The arrest, and subsequent imprisonment, of large numbers of leaders during and at the end of the 1921 dispute was an event which was to recur in 1925 and 1926. In 1921, hundreds of miners were brought before Assize Courts, charged with unlawful assembly associated with the mass picketing of 'safety-men'.

In the localised strike of anthracite miners in West Wales in the summer of 1925, police had to be imported to try to control marching gangs who successfully spread the strike and to escort scabs into work. The subsequent mass trials saw 198 miners charged and 59 eventually imprisoned. Nearly fifty years later, one of the participants, Jim Phillips of Ammanford, expressed the jaundiced view of many towards the way the law was used against the miners who were only trying to maintain a living wage through the protection of their trade union:

> ... the law is always on their side ... the owners. When it comes to a question of a court, it's the same as Justice

Matthew once said, 'the law courts of Britain are open to all, like the doors of the Ritz Hotel'.

The greatest use of police, troops and the courts of law in the South Wales coalfield during the whole of the twentieth century (until possibly 1984–85) occurred during the General Strike and Miners' Lockout of 1926. So overwhelming was the workers' response in South Wales to the call to support the miners that a situation of 'Dual Power' existed during the nine days. In order to regain a sense of authority, central government felt it necessary to introduce troops, a naval presence and the swearing in of special constables. Three battleships and a submarine were moved into South Wales ports.

After the collapse of the General Strike, the character of the miners' fight turned on the continued struggle between central government and its allies (the press, the coal owners, imported police and scabs) and the miners' union and its allies (Labour local authorities, Boards of Guardians, co-operative societies, their political parties and distress committees). In a community under siege, there was no real choice. A community conscious-ness became a class consciousness. There were many kinds of collective forms of support: community soup kitchens, jazz and comic bands, organised coal picking and outcropping, fund-raising by bands and choirs, co-operative boot repairing centres and eventually the ostracising of scabs and even rioting.

The introduction of imported police into the coalfield coincided with the coordinated attempt by the coal owners to accelerate a return to work through intimidation (threats of job losses) and the encouragement of a breakaway scab union. For a coalfield that had hitherto been largely peaceful this was both revealing and offensive. It also proved an enduring memory, with intense feelings against strike-breakers being expressed in 1984–85, especially in those communities divided in the inter-war period.

Such 'interference' manifested itself in many ways across the coalfield under the cloak of the Emergency Powers Regulations. Apart from beatings of individual miners by imported police on their arrival at a mining village, Chief Constables took it upon themselves to ban protest marches to Boards of Guardians, public demonstrations against scabs, surveillance and even public meetings. In 1926, large numbers of police were brought into Pencoed, the very area where the first break in the 1984–85 strike occurred. The then Chief Constable, Lindsay, admitted that Pencoed had been 'ringed off' to forbid meetings owing to a Home Office intimation of 'certain influences at work from London'.

From November onwards, there was a continuation of aggressive managerial tactics and well co-ordinated police protection of scabs (many of whom were intimidated back to work). Sensationalised newspaper reporting at the time attempted to criminalise whole mining communities. Dozens of striking miners and their wives who appeared at the Assize Courts accused mainly of intimidation and unlawful assembly were invariably found guilty, often solely on police evidence: a pattern which was to be repeated many times in disturbances in the Depression years of the 1930s.

The leaders of such disturbances were men and women of standing in the community – checkweighers, chapel deacons, Sunday school teachers, councillors and miners' agents who were witnessing their communities being crushed by the full weight of the state apparatus.

The most celebrated case was Arthur Jenkins, county councillor, justice of the peace and miners' agent, who was alleged to have been the instigator of a riot near Pontypool. Sentencing him to nine months in prison, the judge, as if passing sentence on the unsuitability and role of Labour and the Miners' Federation in the valleys said:

> 'Your position is deplorable. You were a man of high position ... and it was above all things your duty as a public man ... to have assisted the police and maintained order.

Allegations of police violence and drunkenness were made in the House of Commons by South Wales Labour MPs. The behaviour of imported police at Phillipstown and Abercwmboi was so serious that they were investigated by a Home Office Inspector, Sir Leonard Dunning. The significance of the complaints was that the police enjoyed very wide powers under the Emergency Regulations.

What was important about 1926 was that mining communities remained so loyal to their cause for so long. To the great surprise of those who administered the law, an unbreakable spirit survived the lockout. Daniel Lleufer Thomas, a stipendiary magistrate, demanded submission:

> With the settlement of this unfortunate industrial dispute one would expect everyone to submit instead of carrying on at Mardy what is, after all, a sort of guerrilla warfare.

Public pronouncements were one thing. Private comments were another matter altogether. Lindsay, the Chief Constable, must have thought he had had the last word when he wrote glowingly and gloatingly to the Chief Constable of Brighton on the very day the British miners finally accepted defeat:

> I am delighted that your splendid fellows have got home safely. You did indeed send us a capital lot.... They were

easily top-dog in every encounter they had with the strikers and the way they detected and captured the ambush at Pencoedcae was certainly a high class performance. I little thought that men trained in a fashionable resort like Brighton would have adapted themselves with such alacrity to the rough fighting of the Rhondda Valley....

The years of defeat and depression that followed 1926 witnessed the frequent and often excessive use of police in the industrial and political life of the valleys. The Hunger Marchers, locally and to London, were always harassed, intimidated, prosecuted and sometimes, as in the case of at least one unemployed leader, Will Paynter, framed by the highest officers in the Metropolitan force.

One old miner once summed up 1926: 'It taught us to know our enemies better.'

Having lived through 1984–85 he would have said 'amen' to that and added 'we also learnt who our true friends were', for the received memories of the earlier struggles were not just of endurance but the need to return with dignity and in unity. In 1926, the miners returned humiliated and as a rabble. In 1985, South Wales was the only coalfield in Britain where every pit returned under the collective leadership of the NUM.

By 2009, however, in surveying Wales over the past quarter of a century the central question is whether we still learn from our history, celebrate our collectivism and sense of community and cast off any trace of the culture of the victim.

How It All Began:

1947–84

The coal industry was nationalised by a Labour Government in 1947 as a result of decades of campaigning by the miners' union. From the outset, coal nationalisation was intended to ensure that changes were made by consent and agreement of all those in the industry and that its production was planned and utilised for the benefit of the British people. It was believed that the ruthless exploitation of men and mining, authoritarian management and lack of consultation of the workforce had been buried with the old coal owners.

These principles were consolidated in *The Plan for Coal* of 1974 which was endorsed by the Labour Government, the National Coal Board (NCB) and the mining unions, in particular the National Union of Mineworkers (NUM). Most important of all was the commitment in the Plan (and the subsequent report *Coal for the Future* in 1977) to an expanding industry and the central importance of coal in a planned government energy policy. These were all seen as positive developments when compared with the devastating rundown of the industry by successive governments in the 1960s when cheap oil displaced coal.

But there was an underlying fear in the mid-1970s that even though coal production would expand nationally, the peripheral coalfields of Scotland, Kent, the North-East and South Wales might still suffer closures. This was confirmed by the 1975 Common Market fuel and energy plans to contract production to a European profitable market level. Implicitly this meant the phasing out of the peripheral coalfields. This was underlined by a European Economic Community (EEC) document published in 1982 entitled *The Role for Coal in Community Energy Strategy* which laid great emphasis upon the need to secure massively expanded imports of non-EEC coal. Allied to this was the scale of capital investment and the application of new technology into the English central-block coalfields that would inevitably displace the investment-starved peripheral coalfields, especially in a stagnating or declining coal market.

The return of a Conservative Government in 1979 further altered the scene. Determined that they would not be defeated by the NUM as they had been in 1972 and 1974, the new government began to implement a secret Conservative policy report drafted by Nicholas Ridley MP (which was first leaked in *The Economist* of 27th May, 1978). It discussed the setting up of strict financial targets for nationalised industries and their preparation for piecemeal privatisation. The report anticipated that the miners would be likely to resist such drastic changes and suggested the building up of coal stocks (especially at power stations). It also recommended preparing the way for the importation of coal, encouraging hauliers to recruit non-union drivers, the introduction of dual coal/oil firing in all power stations, the establishment of a large, mobile squad of police to deal with picketing and cutting off the money supply to strikers to make the union finance them.

In October 1979 a leaked Cabinet minute stated that 'a nuclear programme would have the advantage of removing a substantial portion of electricity from disruption by industrial action of coal miners and transport workers'. At the same time the British Steel Corporation announced that it was increasing its coking coal imports to one-fifth in 1979–80 and to half in 1980–81.

In December 1979 plans were announced to construct one nuclear power station per year from 1982 for the next decade, thus increasing the nuclear contribution from 12% to 30% by the end of the 1980s and significantly diminishing reliance on coal.

In the period 1980–82 the Government also made major advances in its anti-trade union policies. The 1980 Employment Act introduced restrictions on picketing and 'secondary' action: its Code of Practice limited picketing to a suggested maximum of six at an entrance. It also made changes to penalise families of strikers by deducting assumed strike pay from the supplementary benefit, whether or not a striker was in receipt of such pay. The 1982 Employment Act made unions financially liable in courts for 'illegal' action and made it harder to determine what industrial action was within the law.

The 1980 Coal Industry Act laid the basis for the Government's attack on the nationalised coal industry. It declared that by 1983–84 all operating grants given to the NCB would be ended and that the NCB would have to make a profit. This was at a time when the general economic situation was worsening with the resulting significant decline in demand for coal from British industry.

Following the return of the Conservatives in the 1983 General Election, the NCB conceded that 65,000 workers would need to be shed for the coal industry to break even in 1987–88. So to carry forward the Government's plans, Ian McGregor, who had as chief executive of the British Steel Corporation (BSC) shed 85,000 workers in 1980–83, was appointed chairman of the NCB in September 1983.

On 1st November, 1983, the NUM imposed an overtime ban against the Board's demand for an agreement to close 'uneconomic' pits.

On 6th March, 1984, the NCB announced to the NUM that it intended to cut 4 million tons capacity and 20,000 jobs within the year, thus breaching the normal practice of consultation and agreement in the industry and finally revealing the abandonment of the expansion outlined in *The Plan for Coal*.

The strike action in South Wales and elsewhere in the British coalfields could have been anticipated. The fear of semi-permanent mass unemployment and the attack on trade union rights as represented later in the policing of the strike were concerns which had manifested themselves increasingly since 1979, particularly in South Wales.

The final closure of Deep Dyffryn Colliery in the Cynon Valley in the summer of 1979 had signalled a new awakening in the South Wales coalfield. A broad-based community campaign had been launched by the NUM over the closure, which climaxed with the threat of national industrial action. Again, in 1980 with the rapid rundown of the steel industry in South Wales, although no significant industrial action was achieved, there was a major campaign to educate the workforce as to the imminence of mass pit closures. When the NCB announced its plans to close between 20 and 50 pits in 1981, the spontaneous strikes in South Wales followed by action in other coalfields led to the Government temporarily backing down and withdrawing closure threats, at least for the time being.

Further industrial action against job losses in 1983 in the South Wales pits proved abortive. However, the nature of the resistance in the South Wales coalfield in the whole period of 1979–84 indicated that there had been a growing awareness of the threat to jobs, pits and communities. In this whole period, then, NUM activists in the South Wales coalfield appeared to be in a state of semi-permanent mobilisation.

When the 1984 strike began, the major concerns in South Wales were fourfold. Firstly, there was the need to utilise for the benefit of the people the vast and valuable resources of coal in Wales, irrespective of narrow, short-term 'economic' reasons. Arguments concerning 'economic' pits were considered to be largely irrelevant, even though 'the world may be awash with coal', when so much of it was heavily subsidised as in Poland or produced in 'slave' apartheid conditions as in South Africa. The great reserves of prime coking coal and Europe's unique anthracite reserves in West Wales were ripe for exploitation (as indicated by the opencast sites and the rash of small private mines). The multinational energy companies were waiting for their opportunity. What was needed instead, according to the NUM, was a sane energy policy which used coal and other fuels for the good of the people and not the short-term financial profit of the few.

Secondly, it had been calculated that unemployment in Wales would rise to well over 20% and in mining communities over half the male population would be out of work. The long-term effect of the Government's plans would be that only three pits would be left in Wales, 20,000 mining jobs would go and a further 20,000 would be lost in related industries and services. Mining communities would not survive. There was little prospect of alternative work being introduced, as the record of past governments revealed. There would be an increase in physical and mental illness, suicides, domestic violence and the break-up of families. The valleys of South Wales would be nothing more than an ageing, dying community fit only for tourism and industrial museums.

Thirdly, it was argued that the contraction of the coal industry and the expansion of the nuclear power industry would result, according to the NUM, in the use of a fuel that would be unsafe, inefficient and expensive. The extension of the nuclear programme would result, the NUM believed, in the further restriction of civil liberties because of the power central government and multinational companies would have over energy supply and generation. Its direct relationship to the nuclear weapons industry was also considered to be seen as a threat to democracy and peace.

Finally, if the rundown of the industry were achieved, it would dramatically undermine the power of the NUM and all that it represented. It would, it was argued, lead inevitably to a decline in safety standards down to the levels that already existed in South Africa and the USA. The miners' union in South Wales also had a record second to none over many decades in its concern for its communities, the cultural and educational heritage of Wales and all those who struggled for peace and justice throughout the world.

That is why the union commanded such loyalty from its members and from its communities in the run-up to the strike, as well as from a range of people and organisations throughout Wales.

Few of those involved could have been aware of the full import of what was being embarked upon during March and early April 1984, as the strike gradually got underway. For many observers, the NUM's response to the NCB's announcement on 6th March 1984 of a cut in national capacity of eight million tons per annum and, more immediately, of the imminent closure of the

Cortonwood Colliery in Yorkshire merely confirmed a stereotype of the miners' historical role in opposing Conservative governments. The successes of the national strikes of 1972 and 1974 were rehearsed and shadowier memories of earlier heroic struggles recalled.

What soon became apparent, however, was that the conflict of 1984–85 was different from earlier disputes. Crucially, much more so than before, the conditions in which the strike developed, and was played out, varied radically between the different areas of the British coalfield. Most obviously, of course, Nottingham pursued its own course. However, the very drama of Nottingham's decision not to strike and the consequent clashes between pickets and the police served to obscure the fact that, deprived of the potentially unifying objective of a wages struggle (as had been the case in 1972 and 1974), the unity between the other areas was highly precarious. Simply put, the restructuring of the industry since nationalisation had severely weakened the commonality of interests between the peripheral areas and the central bloc of Yorkshire and the Midlands, and the miners' union had been unable to develop a political strategy sufficiently powerful to compensate for this. It was this, in turn, that underpinned the divisions and conflicts which came to characterise the strike not only at the level of the NUM's national decision-making, but at the grass roots too.

It is against this background, then, that the full significance of the experience of the strike in South Wales should be judged. As is well known, the South Wales Area, on the one hand, remained the most solid and united of all coalfields for the whole of the dispute; on the other, it was crucial in bringing the conflict to an end nearly a year later.

That this militant tradition endured at all is remarkable,

given the massive changes which had occurred in South Wales. In the quarter of a century prior to the strike, the area had suffered as catastrophic a decline as any area of the British coalfield.

Employment & Output (tons) of the South Wales Coalfield

Year	Employment	Output
1948	108,000	23,913,000
1958	99,000	22,822,000
1968	48,000	14,505,748
1978	27,384	7,624,876
1984	20,347	6,720,000

a. Year ending 31 March.
b. Estimate in the absence of the overtime ban.
Source: NCB (South Wales).

Since the late 1950s, coal mining in South Wales had therefore declined in importance in every respect. During the 1960s and earlier 1970s, when so many collieries were being closed, alternative jobs in manufacturing industries had grown in the region. More significantly in numerical terms, there had been a substantial expansion of employment in the services right up until the end of the 1970s. In consequence, by the eve of the strike, even in the coalfield itself, many more people were employed outside the coal industry than in it; in fact, although the NCB remained the largest single employer in South Wales, there were more jobs in, for example, mechanical and electrical engineering or in local government than in coal mining. Equally, however, the severe recession of the late 1970s and early 1980s had wreaked havoc on many of these other industries too. The British Steel Corporation's 'rationalisation' strategy had resulted in the loss of almost 15,000 jobs from the region whilst other manufacturing firms (some of which had established plants in South Wales only as recently as the 1960s) also lost substantial numbers of jobs overall. By the 1980s, even the growth of the services sector had ground to a halt.

One consequence of these changes was that localities that had formerly been almost wholly dependent upon the coal industry had, in effect, had their raison d'etre removed. The upper Afan Valley, in the western part of the coalfield, for example, had seen its last colliery, in Glyncorrwg, close in 1970; by 1984, only thirty-five miners remained in the village, travelling daily to pits in other valleys. For other communities, although coal mining remained a very significant source of jobs, the prospect of further job losses from the industry raised the spectre of a similar, dismal fate. Blaenau Gwent, on the north-eastern rim of the coalfield, still had three pits and one workshop before the strike, providing in excess of 2,000 jobs. However, it had already lost some 7,000 jobs during the previous decade in the rundown of the steel industry. Official figures showed that total unemployment in the area stood at over 20%, with male unemployment at almost 25% and that for women at 14%. If half the mining jobs were to be lost, the male rate would rise to almost 31% (including the 'knock-on' effects). Moreover, to this could be added a further 10% of the workforce engaged in temporary employment.

The South Wales valleys in the mid-1980s were ageing and declining: characterised by new mining museums and new old people's homes, as well as pit, school and hospital closures. Such a grim picture was common to all the threatened peripheral coalfields of Britain when the NCB closure programme was announced. However, two factors set South Wales apart. Firstly, it had suffered from a chronic lack of investment in its specialised, high-quality coals, even though there was, for example, a world shortage of anthracite. In 1982, a meagre £7.63 million had been allocated to construct new capacity and facilitate coal treatment, compared with £453.5 million for North Yorkshire, whilst even the Western Area received £75.7 million. Accordingly, the impact of the proposed closures was expected to be especially severe. Indeed, it was claimed the cutback would entail a loss of some 500,000 tons of output in South Wales and the eventual reduction of the coalfield to six collieries.

Secondly, having learned the lessons of the savage closures of the 1960s, the South Wales Area of the NUM had tried to adopt a strategy of combativeness in defence of pits and the coalfield communities. Ever since the late 1970s, the NUM leadership had worked to prepare the membership for a final showdown with the NCB and ultimately the Government, again drawing upon the potent imagery of the radical past. Emlyn Williams, the Area President, in his 1983 Annual Address, put it this way:

> Our reputation as political leaders in the British coalfields built by Arthur Horner, Bill Paynter and Dai Francis, is at stake.

The Times, addressing a rather different audience three years earlier, had come to the same conclusion:

> What we are shortly to see in South Wales is not just the latest battle over factory shutdowns, but the trial of the ideological basis of the 'shock troops' of the trade union movement. (8th July, 1980)

The battle for Deep Duffryn Colliery in 1978–79 had been a watershed for, although it had ended in defeat, it had in many respects heralded a new era. For the first time, saving a pit was explicitly linked to the fate of its dependent community, presaging the arguments which would come to play such a significant part in the events of 1984–85. The local mobilisation of community groups, as well as nearby collieries, similarly prefigured elements of the 'community socialism' which was to be expressed so much more forcefully in the later, national conflict.

The Deep Duffryn campaign jerked the 1979 National Annual Conference of the NUM into making a declaration in support of industrial action. Again the following year, the Area leadership attempted to mobilise solidarity action in defence of steel jobs. They failed, but the attempt provided valuable lessons for the spectacular, if temporary, success of the February 1981 strike. Starting unofficially in South Wales, the strike spread to several coalfields and resulted in a complete U-turn on the closure programme proposed by the Thatcher government. A similar spontaneous action in 1983, begun by a stay-in strike in defence of the Lewis Merthyr Colliery, resulted in thousands of South Wales activists 'lobbying' every pit in Britain. This unique, if sobering, experience, despite the dismal defeat of the subsequent national ballot, had prepared them for the coming storm, for they had been almost totally isolated in their struggle.

By March 1984, however, the vastly different levels of coalfield investment, as well as the widening disparities between wage levels made possible by the 1977–78 incentive scheme, had accentuated the divergences between the interests of the different areas. The construction of a viable consensus in support of industrial action was thus going to be even more difficult than on previous occasions.

The militant coalfields had long understood that no successful strike could be contemplated without the full and active support of the biggest coalfield, Yorkshire, whose left-wing credentials were being questioned, as were those of its protégé, the national president Arthur Scargill, following his apparent hesitancy in the brief disputes of 1981 and 1983.

The opportunity to kick-start a wide-ranging struggle against pit closures came with what the distinguished industrial correspondent Geoffrey Goodman called a 'monumental shock' with the announced closure of Yorkshire's Cortonwood Colliery on 1st March. The suspicion within the NUM was that Ian McGregor was tiring of a gradualist and conciliatory approach. The leadership of the Yorkshire Area of the NUM accepted the challenge provided by Cortonwood as an opportunity to mobilise all the British coalfields. And it was this grave proposition that was unexpectedly being considered by miners in South Wales in the early days of March, a most unlikely time as winter was coming to a close.

Even within South Wales it was quite clear in the Area conference on 9th March that many delegates had grave doubts as to whether they could persuade their members to take industrial action. Their Area Executive Council was recommending an indefinite strike, without a ballot, on the basis of the 68% mandate from 1983. It was also asking for endorsement in the light of the National Executive's decision to authorise and support Area strikes, allowed for without national ballot under rule 41. There were several in the Area conference who preferred to continue the overtime ban which had already been operating for eighteen weeks, but the overwhelming majority (only five lodges voted against) accepted Emlyn Williams' argument that the coalfield was in a completely new situation.

Back in the coalfield, however, it was a rather different matter. There was confusion and some strange reactions. Oakdale and

Betws, long-life pits at opposite ends of the coalfield, with no tradition of militancy, voted for action. Of the majority that voted against industrial action, many were themselves threatened with closure (St John's at Maesteg was a prime example). In part, this was the result of the demoralising defeat of 1983. In addition, news of votes against action spread to meetings which had not yet decided, with the obvious negative result (as, for example, at Cwm and Merthyr Vale). There was also genuine confusion over whether the 1983 mandate still applied and whether there should be a show of hands, an area ballot or a national one; or were they being instructed to come out?

What happened at the Roseheyworth Lodge (Abertillery) could well have summed up the problem. The lodge minutes record (10th March 1984):

> ... the EC would rather lead than surrender. The ballot result in 1983 is still valid. On many occasions the men asked for either a vote or a ballot. It was stated that the conference had already decided that we were on strike. The meeting was very stormy, men declaring that they were going to work. They were told we are on strike. Dai Flower got up and unofficially asked the men to vote on who wanted to work, the men got up and left the hall, duration of the meeting was 2 hours.

What occurred between then and the following Monday is of crucial significance to an understanding of the subsequent strike in South Wales. The Roseheyworth minutes again:

> Monday morning 12th March, 1984. Lodge officers meet the men in the canteen and all went home except 32, after the day shift no other men worked except safety men.

At 1.30 p.m. on Sunday, 11th March the dormant 'broad left' activists met in the Ambulance Hall at Hirwaun. They were 'veterans' of previous 'unofficial' movements since 1969 and were drawn essentially from the most militant lodges, invariably from the centre of the coalfield – Maerdy, Tower, Treforgan, Trelewis Drift and Aberpergwm and later joined by other lodges, notably Penrhiwceiber. They were the rump of a 'broad left' which had apparently been broken by the 1983 defeat. The prospect before them was a daunting one, but they decided to picket the whole coalfield even if only one pit had voted for action. The coalfield was quickly divided up accordingly.

By the time the Executive Council was meeting at Pontypridd on Monday morning (12th March), Maerdy and Tower pickets, with their banners, were already there to meet them. It was clear that Yorkshire was out en bloc and picketing in South Wales had been largely successful. Encouraged by these developments, the Executive Council took the most important decisions in its history:

1. The Miners' Agents convene mass committee meetings in their areas tomorrow morning.
2. A strike committee be formed from the executive consisting of one executive council member for each of the zones plus the two craftsmen's representatives.
3. We reaffirm our policy and that the following press statement be made:

The South Wales area executive council having received an updated report of the situation in the coalfield this morning, unanimously decided to call on all our members to declare their unanimous support for those of our members who are carrying out conference decisions. We

thank all our members who have made this sacrifice to
stop the destruction of the South Wales coalfield.

The way in which South Wales came to be on strike in March
1984 provides some critical clues about the subsequent course
of events. The often acrimonious union meetings of 10th–11th
March and during the following week highlighted the
precariousness of unity at local and national levels. One such
meeting took place at Pyle, Mid Glamorgan.

The Pyle Leisure Centre was an unlikely venue for a miners'
strike meeting. On the morning of Tuesday, 13th March, 1984
it was particularly odd, as most of the miners present represented lodges in the Maesteg and Swansea districts, which
had voted against strike action. It was an inauspicious start to
the longest strike in South Wales and British mining history.
Yorkshire, Kent and Scotland had already struck and seemed
solid. Durham was almost entirely out, and two pits in
Nottingham were said to have been 'convinced'. Yet the two
Blaenant delegates at the back of the hall refused (with many
others) to clap when two representatives from Kent were
welcomed. Three out of the five executive members on the
platform had failed to carry their own lodges and the miners'
agent himself had failed to sway the general meeting at Cwm,
one of the biggest pits in the coalfield. The atmosphere was
sullen, confused, angry. There were private mutterings of
'Yorkshire owes us a fortnight, make them sweat' from those
who said they had 'seen it all before in 1983' and that a
national struggle needed a national ballot.

The uncertainty began to fade when it became apparent that
if South Wales struck, it would not be doing so in glorious
isolation. A young miner from Kent focused precisely on the
problem:

23

I was born in Brithdir in the Rhymney Valley thirty years ago. My parents moved to Kent in search of wor ... I am not down to picket... There has always been a close bond between our coalfields of mutual benefit. We in Kent face problems. It is a depressed area similar to South Wales... If we show a weakness now, they will exploit us. It will be a disaster if you don't back us... We've got Yorkshire out, at last.... It is to the credit of your area that the overwhelming number of your members are already out. They have lived up to their militant traditions and I salute you for it.

That was not what Hefina Headon, later one of the outstanding leaders of the support groups on the coalfield, said to her husband, John, the previous day when he had come home on strike: 'You're twenty years too late. You should have done it when they shut Seven Colliery....'

By the weekend, the uncertainty had passed. The overwhelming fear of isolation had gone. Every lodge was, somehow, in support of the strike and by the Sunday night, South Wales was on the offensive, with thousands of its members already on their way to 'lobby' other coalfields, and soon afterwards to power stations and cities throughout most of Britain.

Eighteen of its twenty-eight pits had originally voted against action, but within less than a week the position had been reversed by further general meetings. Every South Wales miner was on strike, and their coalfield was to be the most solid for the duration of the year-long dispute. The story of that turn-around in South Wales in that first week was rooted as much in the past as in the immediate crisis. Arguably, the coalfield had been the most consistently militant in Britain ever since the turn of the century and for decades the union had had a

Communist-Left Labour leadership. This had given rise to a powerful sense of the importance of a particular historical legacy. Reflecting on the solidarity of 1984–85, the future president of the Area, Des Dutfield, described the significance of this '... tradition, background ... ancestry. Call it what you like. It's always been a fact of life as far as I've known the industry: fathers, grandfathers before me and now my son.'

Nevertheless, by Wednesday, 14th March, although the stoppage was already total in South Wales, there was still a handful of lodges that had not officially voted for strike action. At South Celynen, in Gwent, Ray Lawrence, the lodge secretary, had a particularly daunting task. One of only three to picket on the first morning, his pit had been resisting closure for years, with a nine-week overtime ban in 1981 and a three-week strike in 1983 over lack of recruitment. It had been a long, lonely and difficult battle which had come to a head three weeks before the start of the strike when the pit had been put into the review procedure. Lawrence's men and their families had already been worn down by closure worries. A mixture of deep pessimism, genuine concerns about lack of democratic consultation and a fear of acting in isolation from other coalfields had a bearing on South Celynen's opposition to strike action.

All this was swept to one side, however, with some forthright and occasionally vigorous picketing. But such action could not force men out on strike. Clearly, the decisive leadership provided by the Area rank-and-file Executive Council and its officials played an important part. Equally, the very obvious national momentum of strike action conveyed by the media created an optimistic atmosphere. But most important of all – particularly amongst miners who were not activists – was what Ray Lawrence described as '... the tremendous loyalty to the union ingrained in them from generations past ... and also ...

the personal loyalty to lodge officers'. It was crucial, then, that there had been no organised opposition to the strike among lodge and area officials, who not only abided by long-established policy decisions, arrived at by ballot and conference, but also went on to the immediate offensive.

The strike had begun. Crucially, very few South Wales miners were prepared to cross what were, for the most part, only token picket lines. By the end of the week, all coal production and coal movement had been halted and South Wales pickets were already fanning out all over the country. With one eye on the new picketing laws, Emlyn Williams was very happy to be reported in *The Western Mail* (17th March, 1984) as saying:

[South Wales pickets in other coalfields were] a complete surprise. I have been travelling across the coalfield extensively and I didn't know anything about it... They obviously consulted well with each other and moved quickly – a good tactic but they certainly didn't act on any executive instruction or advice.

On that first Wednesday (14th March), the Crumlin NUM office, responsible for the Eastern (Gwent and Rhymney) part of the coalfield, was already bursting with volunteers eager to play their part, now that their lodges had, in effect, reversed their earlier decisions. Pickets were being sent on rota to local power stations and even out into the English coalfields. One forty-seven-year-old was heard to say at the local Institute: 'Well, I'm against a strike. I just can't afford it. But once we're into it, well, it's a different matter then.' He had a twenty-two-year-old son who had never worked. 'I'm goin' to Leicester for him,' he said.

It was a combination of loyalty to the union and a determination to honour family bonds that characterised the strike throughout South Wales for the next twelve months.

The Strike as a New Kind of Politics?

March–October 1984

After the strike was over, many South Wales activists felt that they had lived through four strikes not one: an industrial dispute, albeit an abnormal one, with the full weight of the state apparatus being used against them from the earliest days (March until the end of July 1984); 'a way of life', from the moment of sequestration on 1st August until mid-November 1984, when there were the first returns to work; 'defending the coalfield', with the return of the bulk of the picketing and collecting activists to stave off a mass return to work (mid-November 1984 until the end of January 1985); and, finally, 'saving the union', during the last month, when the original aim of the strike became secondary to protecting the NUM itself from disintegration. But each distinct period could be described as being part of a new kind of politics.

Picketing was the dominant feature of the strike in South Wales during the first month. From the end of the first week until the need arose to feed children during the various school half-term holidays, picketing, by traditional definitions, made the struggle very much a male phenomenon, with an estimated four to five thousand South Wales NUM members (or about 25% of the workforce) permanently mobilised. Apart from this relatively high level of activism, what was also impressive was its discipline, organisation and dynamism. All picketing was organised from the Area Headquarters at Pontypridd by the research officer, Kim Howells, who was responsible to the Area Executive Council and its officials. The size of the operation was breathtaking.

Despite police surveillance, police roadblocks, police warnings to coach operators and massive police presence at English coalfields and other NUM targets, by the end of March, South Wales had pickets throughout the coalfields of Lancashire, Nottingham, Warwick, South Derby, Leicester, Stafford and North Wales; it was picketing or monitoring twenty-six nuclear, coal and oil power stations as far afield as Wylfa (Gwynedd), Didcot (Oxfordshire), Fawley (Hampshire) and Tilbury (Essex); it was manning six regional centres that ultimately became the focal points for fundraising and propaganda at Birmingham, Swindon, Southampton, Worcester, Crewe and Devon; and there were four other centres primed to attack random targets. The exercise was intensified in May, with ports on the Essex coast being picketed and a team even being sent over to the Dutch ports to monitor coal movements at Rotterdam and Amsterdam. All this indicated a desire for a quick tactical victory, once it had become clear that the Nottingham miners were not to be picketed out and that a successful, nationally co-ordinated strategy was going to be extremely difficult to achieve. The financial costs were astronomical at more than £35,000 per week; £1 million had been spent in the major mobilisation of the first six weeks, according to a report in the *South Wales Echo* on 19th April, 1984. There was also the human cost: constant activity could not be maintained for weeks on end, particularly with dwindling numbers following arrests and frightening confrontations with the police.

But in the early weeks this intense and dynamic industrial strategy seemed to be justified. A combination of long-distance travelling to the English coalfields and the experience of past struggles resulted in a distinctive South Wales style of picketing, very different from the confrontational mass picketing engaged in by the Yorkshire miners in particular. By 20th March most of the North Wales miners had been picketed out and smaller successes were being achieved in Staffordshire and Warwickshire. Even earlier, coal trains had been stopped from going into power stations in South Wales and Didcot, as a result of the solidarity of the rail unions, ASLEF and the NUR, along with the Transport and General Workers' Union (TGWU) members inside the plants themselves. Nevertheless, arrests and strict bail conditions were taking their toll, especially on the more militant lodges in the centre of the coalfield. Maerdy, with nearly half of its membership of 690 miners mobilised at this time, saw itself as '... the tip of a spear launched against collieries elsewhere'.

The strike was not going to be won by South Wales alone, however active it was in picketing beyond its own coalfield. As early as 21st March the Wales Trades Union Congress (TUC) acceded to a request from the South Wales Area of the NUM for 'full support'. This was the first attempt to broaden the struggle and resulted in major rallies at Cardiff on 28th April and 12th June. One was also held at Wrexham. The latter coincided with a Wales TUC 'Day of Action', called in defiance of the British TUC, which undoubtedly helped to undermine its effectiveness. Assisted by the Wales TUC, attempts in these early months to limit coal and coke movements into Llanwern and Port Talbot steelworks failed not because of any unwillingness to agree locally (in fact, an agreement was achieved at Llanwern), but because the NUM national president, Arthur Scargill, insisted that all agreements should be national ones and that unless this was achieved by midnight 19th June, all supplies should be stopped. The cautious South Wales approach had been aimed at winning the support of the steelworkers by showing a desire to protect steel jobs. The result of the nationally imposed strategy was the disaster of the scab convoy of over a hundred giant lorries, roaring daily along the M4 from Port Talbot (with its deep-water harbour) to Llanwern for the remainder of the strike. Instead of achieving a probable limitation of coal and coke supplies, steel production in fact rocketed in South Wales and a serious breach was made in a vital industrial alliance. The failure to win over the steelworkers was to result in a further, equally serious setback for the South Wales miners some months later, when their funds were frozen for being in breach of a court order to stop secondary picketing.

By the end of April there was talk in the coalfield of going through the first 'pain barrier', as the strike extended beyond those of 1972 and 1974. The coalfield was entering uncharted waters, at least for the present generation. As the weeks slipped by, the talk was then about 'How did they survive the 1926 strike?' and, increasingly, of 'the need for an army to march on its stomach'. At the very same time, half-term holidays spurred local initiatives to feed children, as did the first National Women's Rally held on 12th May, 1984. South Wales women, most of whom had never visited another coalfield before, returned from the rally determined to play their full part, as they perceived it then, in the evolving struggle. One Seven Sisters woman came back to tell local lodge activists that '... women are not going to be "simpled" anymore', after she and her group had seen the levels of organisation amongst women in South Yorkshire.

Initially, this new role involved the extension of women's traditional domestic responsibilities from the family to the wider stage of community provision through the food centres. And for many women, this remained the predominant experience of the strike. However, it became evident that a more far-reaching mobilisation of whole communities was necessary to prevent the collapse of the strike, and women were to play a key role in this wider mobilisation as organisers, fund-raisers and political propagandists. The creation in June of a coalfield-wide organisation, the South Wales Women's Support Group, provided the institutional vehicle for co-ordinating and increasing this invaluable activity including the lobbying and picketing of the Welsh Office on the issue of benefits for striking miners' families.

The first warning of a weakening of the strike came in the tenth week at Cynheidre Colliery, in the far western Gwendraeth Valley in the anthracite coalfield. Although fundraising had started there, it was at a very early stage and the threat of a return to work was helped by a lack of proper local community and women's involvement. The breakaway was defeated through a rapid, coalfield-wide response, involving a picket that included a delegation of women from the Dulais Valley, who arrived triumphantly despite police roadblocks. This was followed by a rally at Pontyberem on 26th May, with representatives from all over South Wales, Leicestershire striking miners, the Dyfed Farmers Action Group (which provided, then and later, milk for miners' families) and a wide range of political and community organisations.

As the food collecting and fund-raising began to gather momentum in April and May, so also the nature of the strike imperceptibly began to change. Support for the strike began to spread not only through the dense social networks of the coalfield communities themselves, but also outwards beyond the coalfield to extended families and friends, to former mineworkers and, ultimately, to a wide range of supporters. It began to be conceivable that this broadly based alliance could draw on a sufficiently rich vein of financial and moral support and that the NCB and the Thatcher government could be isolated politically.

Certainly, by June there was a growing realisation within the NUM and throughout striking mining communities that if any success was to be achieved, it would be a long haul, possibly through to winter. The intransigence of Nottingham and other working coalfields and the determination of the government to use all its powers against the strike produced an equal and opposite determination in the South Wales valleys. The cut of the £15 per week social security benefit to strikers' families and the severity of police action at Orgreave in June were both sobering lessons for activists and non-activists alike, which unified rather than divided communities.

Quite spontaneously, then, food collections and fundraising began and spread; they were an important political gesture of solidarity for those who had previously been unable to show support inside and beyond the coalfield. This support also came to be seen as a way for the NUM itself to show, in the absence of official strike pay, that it was concerned with the plight of its members and their families. Even before the South Wales Area Executive Council took a decision at the end of April to call on its three principal centres, based at Ammanford (West Wales), Pontypridd (the Central Valleys) and Crumlin (Gwent and Rhymney), to set up food centres, a variety of local initiatives had been taken. The tardiness of the union in taking on this work can in part be explained by a genuine belief that food distribution would result in a 'settling down' to a static strike, with 'over-fed' activists unable even to play football on picket lines. That scepticism melted away as the striking miners were engulfed in a rising tide of emerging support groups.

The variety of different roots put down in so many parts of the coalfield added to the subsequent strength of the strike. The earliest report of food collections was noted on 13th April by the Oakdale NUM Lodge: their factory collections eventually grew into a massive operation with tentacles worldwide (at least according to envious and admiring neighbouring valleys) in the shape of the Gwent Food Fund. In Blaenau Gwent, it was the Borough Council, with a £10 food voucher for every family, that showed a lead. In Treherbert, in the Rhondda, it was the Communist Party that played the key role; in Bridgend, the Labour MP Ray Powell offered his local headquarters as a focal point: 'I suppose you could call it a modern day soup kitchen – but it is only borrowing ideas which have existed for well over fifty years.' In the Dulais Valley, it was a coalescing of emerging women's groups, Community Councils, the Neath Trade Council and Borough Council, Communists, members of the Labour Party and the strike committee itself which set up a distribution network covering eventually three valleys and over a thousand families. In the capital city, the Cathays Ward Labour Party Miners' Support Group was able to announce that after twenty weeks £2,000 had been collected, along with a great deal of food; its leaflet announced '9 May Street, 6.30pm meeting Tues., Wed., Thurs., no sectarianism – all welcome'.

Beyond the coalfield, South Wales pickets were already, by this time, establishing support groups to raise funds. At Oxford, the groundwork already done by Kent miners, a support group (with car workers and students especially active) was developed by Maerdy and Merthyr Vale pickets at Didcot power station. A range of political organisations combined with local pickets at the nuclear power stations of Wylfa and Trawsfynydd to twin the communities of Ynys Môn, Bangor and Blaenau Ffestiniog with West Wales mining communities: local Communists, Cymdeithas yr Iaith Gymraeg (the Welsh Language Society), Plaid Cymru, Labour Party activists and the Bangor Socialist Society were particularly prominent in such areas. Eventually all these diverse bodies and organisations came together to form the North Wales Congress in Support of Mining Communities.

The long-term political implications of these support networks were not fully appreciated in Britain at the time and certainly not by NUM officials in South Wales, who were justifiably concerned that the extent of their activities (compared with other parts of the NUM) was placing a disproportionate financial burden on their Area. By the middle of May, every mining village and town in South Wales had its own community-based or women's support group, and gradually through the summer support organisations evolved in the adjoining coastal cities of Cardiff and Swansea (where a sprinkling of miners' families were still located). The die then seemed cast for an exceptionally long strike. To save money the annual Miners' Gala, Miners' Eisteddfod and the Annual Conference were all cancelled. Special efforts were made to provide every miner's child with a holiday, and prominent lodge activists, Charlie White of St John's and Tony Taylor of Coedely, were drafted into the Area Office to organise them.

By early August, children of striking miners were being sent on holiday to Belgium (8), France (28), Switzerland (20) and Ireland (50). There were twenty-seven with the Cymdeithas Yr Iaith, which also organised a coach trip to the National Eisteddfod. There were plans for groups to go to Spain and Austria whilst the SOGAT print union sent thirty-two children to Rottingdean in Sussex.

Charlie White and Tony Taylor undertook a survey of where South Wales pickets were establishing support groups, mainly across the South of England but also further afield. There was a joke doing the rounds that Arthur Scargill's antipathy to South Wales meant 'we were given Ireland' whilst Kent and Nottingham were 'given the whole of London and North America'. That 'joke' was used as a challenge to reach out imaginatively, 'below the radar', beyond the traditional labour movement, into churches and peace groups, women's groups, indeed any progressive grouping.

The survey revealed that virtually every NUM lodge was involved in this kind of solidarity work. Cynheidre was in Redditch, Bodmin; ASLEF in East London, Bristol and Luton; Betws and Abernant were in Brixton and Lambeth; Maerdy was in Oxford, Birmingham and Bristol; Merthyr Vale in Didcot, Preston, Liverpool; and most impressively, almost as a foretaste of the 1990s, Tower was in Islington, Fleet Street, Liverpool, Yeovil, Poole and Bournemouth.

An examination of *The Valleys' Star*, the weekly newspaper of the Neath, Dulais and Swansea Valleys' Miners Support Group, showed a remarkable range of elaborate connections locally and worldwide. Its Christmas edition reported support from Hampshire, Swindon, Birmingham, London Gays and Lesbians and *Daily/Sunday Express* NGA chapel which had already donated £15,000 to the local groups.

The long hot summer – 'strike weather' so reminiscent of 1926, 1921 and 1898 – was dominated every weekend from May through to September by local community rallies, almost like carnivals in their atmosphere. Old banners from long-closed collieries were dug out of the archives of the South Wales Miners' Library to haunt the NCB with memorials of its past mismanagement. Women from the coalfield joined peace

36

protesters at the Port Talbot steelworks and at Greenham Common. Union leaders talked in terms of 'no surrender', of 'hell freezing over, before returning to work' and of the 'heroism of the womenfolk'. MPs spoke evocatively of the revival of 'community spirit' in the valleys, whilst children wrote poems about their exciting new experiences, unconsciously recalling the pathos of their grandparents' memories of 1926. Lisa James of Seven Sisters wrote:

They were talking of closures
And shortages of coal
And how all the people
Want work and not dole.
Then we went to the club
To have something to eat.
There were biscuits and crisps
And sandwiches... MEAT!

The people went home
Despondent and sad.
The children played on
With the little they had
On slides and on roundabouts
Swings with a jerk. Maybe tomorrow
our fathers will work.

The collective optimism – at least outwardly – of the valleys was interrupted on 1st August, 1984, when all South Wales Area NUM bank accounts, including its food funds and those of some support groups, were frozen because of the Area's refusal to comply with a court order barring its secondary picketing of Port Talbot steelworks. This was the consequence of South Wales, uniquely, taking the lead in picketing essentially across two-thirds of the landmass of Britain. Sequestration effectively ended this.

The small family firm of Richard and George Reade from the Forest of Dean had successfully taken the NUM (South Wales Area) ·to the High Court for attempting to picket its lorries, which were part of the Port Talbot–Llanwern convoy. There was much speculation, then and subsequently, about the motivation behind a small firm invoking the new Conservative employment legislation, whilst other bigger employers, notably the British Steel Corporation itself, had studiously avoided doing so. Whatever the reasons, the political intent was clear: to neutralise perhaps the most effective picketing machine in the British coalfields and the Area with arguably the greatest local popular support. The sequestration of the funds effectively ended South Wales' picketing activities beyond its own coalfield, but the action of the High Court, rather than demoralising communities and supporters, merely intensified their determination and turned their strike increasingly into a resistance movement and a way of life.

The sequestration of South Wales funds was the final confirmation, if any were necessary, of the seriousness of the state's assault on the miners. It added to the abundant evidence already available from the trauma of the failure of mass picketing to close the coke depot at Orgreave (later called 'Orgrave' by Scottish NUM leader George Bolton). In retrospect, it can be seen to have raised in the most acute fashion the question of the adequacy of the strategy being pursued by the NUM national leadership throughout this early period: a strategy rooted in the attempt to use mass picketing to force a resolution to the dispute. And certainly, after the strike, it became possible for thoughtful NUM leaders, such as the national vice president, Michael

McGahey, to acknowledge that there had been a failure to come to terms with the defeat at Orgreave and at the steelworks; and a crucial confusion of 'Here We Go' rallies – attended overwhelmingly by the committed activists. McGahey publicly said later, 'We confused mass rallies for mass movements.' In private, he was far more critical, calling such strategies 'degenerate syndicalism'. At the time, however, the desperate need for a 'victory', however symbolic, as one defeat followed another, seems to have precluded any genuine strategic debate. The one exception seems to have been the internal South Wales discussion document written by press officer and picket organiser Kim Howells, which was circulated as early as mid-May to all South Wales lodges. It was forthright in its criticism of '... much confusion and lack of direction amongst area and national leaderships...' and focused in particular on the failure to stop coal movements, ineffective picketing, the inability to create a national machinery to feed NUM members and, most damning of all, the lack of any '... formulation of short, simple demands or targets'. It concluded, ominously, on the question of financing areas where the struggle was most intense:

> No one, however, is clear about the role of Sheffield [the NUM national headquarters] in alleviating of the financial burdens. Clarification on this is needed quickly.

The division between 'Sheffield' and the South Wales leadership, so manifest in this important document, was not to surface publicly until January 1985. Throughout 1984, however, the questioning of strategy was of little significance, as the mythology of mass picketing in the style of Saltley Gates in 1972 (which had relied so much on wider trade union solidarity) continued to dominate national and much local thinking.

The tension was at its sharpest over Scargill's call for a complete blockade of steelworks, which destroyed the carefully nurtured solidarity between steel and miners' unions locally.

These very private yet sharp debates over industrial versus political strategies grew and were personified in the two dominant left leaders: Arthur Scargill, a latter-day syndicalist in the tradition of Arthur Cook who focused on mass picketing, and the Communist Michael McGahey who wanted to broaden strategies into a more sophisticated political struggle culminating in a lobby of Parliament which ultimately did take place on 7th June.

Following the sequestration, fundraising and food parcels, rather than picketing, became the dominant feature of the strike. Public campaigning tended to focus more on 'starving children' than on the case for coal. The outward appearance was of a dangerously static, almost comfortable, and yet frenetically exciting, struggle: a struggle which, with increasing public support, could 'go on for ever'. But beneath all the external community confidence was a growing private fear of debt and defeat, which every family carried with fortitude and, for the most part, in silence.

How the South Wales Area of the NUM and its supporting organisations survived another seven months without the use of its own bank accounts had much to do with the strength of popular support for the strike that existed in the valley communities and beyond, as well as with the organisational discipline that permeated what had come to be seen as nothing less than a communal struggle and resistance movement. It is instructive that the most revealing and effective NUM leaflet produced in Wales during the strike declared – in English and Welsh – 'Close a Pit, Kill a Community'; 'Cau Pwll, Lladd Cymuned'.

The immediate impact of sequestration, then, was to clarify the strength of social and institutional relationships within the South Wales valleys. Despite the decades of decline, the social networks structured out of bonds of family and community continued to provide a remarkable resource to be mobilised. The crisis also created conditions in which the prospect of a wider mobilisation became possible, expressing the very special regard in which the South Wales miners were held throughout Wales.

In the week following sequestration, two very different developments illustrated these inter-relationships. Firstly, the attempt by lone miners to return to work ('coinciding' as it did with an orchestrated attempt in all coalfields) following the so-called miners' holidays brought forth a phenomenal and spontaneous community reaction. Neither police nor the NCB, with its laid-on buses, could cope. At Garw, Cwm, Bedwas and Aberaman, individual scabs had to accept defeat in the face of massive community responses; there was even an example of a milkman refusing to deliver to a scab's house. The buses failed to cross picket lines. It was an open secret that South Wales Area Director, Philip Weekes, himself a product of a valley community and clearly out of step with the McGregor management style, was not exactly an enthusiast for the return of the odd miner or two. Further attempts at orchestrated revolts, especially during TUC week in September, likewise foundered on the rock of community resistance.

There were hopes of a negotiated settlement over the summer but they foundered over the definition of 'uneconomic pits'. There were also hopes then, and at various times throughout the strike, of industrial action by the colliery officials' union, NACODS, which was responsible for pit safety. But such hopes were in reality exaggerated because the NUM's unity was so fragile: to depend on NACODS revealed the NUM's own weakness.

41

Compared with other coalfields, then, scab-free South Wales had an air of unreality. Ammanford miners played cricket with policemen although they always switched to Welsh in front of strangers. At South Celynen, the lodge chairman, under the full glare of television cameras, talked out a threatened return to work over a pint of beer. Most dramatically of all, well-organised groups of miners occupied, under cover of darkness, the Newport transporter bridge and the cranes at the deep-water harbour of Port Talbot steelworks, so as to prevent the importation of coking coal – much to the embarrassment of local police.

Simultaneously with these localised developments, in August there was the coalescing of the various progressive threads throughout Wales in support of the miners. This first became evident during the National Eisteddfod at Lampeter, where the National Union of Public Employees (NUPE) and Cymdeithas yr Iaith Gymraeg provided the main fundraising thrust around which a range of cultural and political organisations gathered. Eventually this unity took on an institutional form with the launching by the NUM in South Wales of the Wales Congress in Support of Mining Communities. Endorsed by over three hundred prominent people in Welsh public life, its aims were simple: to increase fundraising by setting up more support groups and to assist the NUM in putting the case for coal. Its principal achievement was that it ensured that the NUM was never isolated within Wales during the coming desperate months. What emerged was a network of unexpected alliances that went far beyond the traditional labour movement. Labour and Plaid Cymru MPs shared platforms and stood on picket lines with women's groups, church leaders, peace and Welsh language activists and, interestingly enough, a gay and lesbian support group from London (which ultimately raised over £28,000 for the coalfield). The involvement of this group mainly through links with the Dulais Valley, was a significant political development with future Labour MP Sian James addressing the 1985 Gay Pride Rally in London, accompanied by a contingent from the Abernant NUM, whose banner led the march.

Equally, however, it was during this period that the Welsh Council of Churches not only publicly identified itself with the plight of the mining communities, but also sought to take initiatives to bring about a 'reconciliation'. Ironically, then, it was from within the only scab-free coalfield in Britain that the notion of the strike 'coming to an end sometime' came about. The effectiveness of fundraising in London, in the southern soft underbelly of England from Cornwall to Southampton and in many parts of the world undoubtedly created an illusion of security in the long run-up to Christmas. But as the strike began to crumble in other coalfields, quiet, uncomfortable questions were being asked back home in food centres, miners' halls and homes along the lines of 'where is the strike going?'. The answer finally came on the morning of Monday, 5th November. The long, bitter retreat had finally reached South Wales.

The Coalfield Under Siege:

November 1984 – March 1985

The most concerted effort at an organised return to work came on Monday, 5th November. Area Director Philip Weekes' reluctance to follow the bullish style of other NCB area directors was finally worn down, by the agitation both from below of a handful of 'super scabs' and from above with the NCB National Board and, it is likely, members of the Cabinet pushing for a breach in the strike's most solid area. Weekes later recalled:

I was still saying that I wanted the men to go back, but trying to phrase my words in such a way that it avoided the individual or small group. I wanted the whole damned lot going back when they went ... And in this I was telling the NUM what I was doing ... But it was a horrible period ... That was the worst of all because I was in a situation of extreme conflict and not too certain of what was the best for anybody.

Wales Congress Aberystwyth Rally, November 1984
Photo by Terry Davies

Dafydd Iwan at NUPE stand singing in support at
Lampeter National Eisteddfod, August 1984
Photo by Hywel Francis

NUM lobby of Parliament, 7th June, 1984
Photo by Hywel Francis

Hywel Francis presents 'Dirty Thirty' in Leicester with The Fed, *April 1984*
Photo by Hywel Francis

Tony Ciano, first right, with fellow committee men in
Cynheidre canteen on first day back, 5th March, 1985
Photo by Hywel Francis

NUM/Wales TUC Cardiff rally, June 1984
Tondu Photo Workshop

Young strike supporters at Maesteg
Tondu Photo Workshop

Women pickets at Port Talbot Steelworks, 1984
Tondu Photo Workshop

London Gays and Lesbians present bus to Neath, Dulais and
Swansea Valleys Miners' Support Group, March 1985
Photo by Imogen Young

Sian James speaking with Arthur Scargill at
All Wales Women's Conference in Caerphilly
Photo by Imogen Young

Dennis Skinner MP, at 1982 South Wales Miners' Gala
Photo by Hywel Francis

Croeserw, Afan Valley supporters at Pontyberem Valley Demonstration,
26th May, 1984
Photo by Hywel Francis

Southampton trade union march led by South Wales NUM banner
South Wales Coalfield Archive

Hampshire supporters give Christmas presents to Cynon Valley families
South Wales Coalfield Archive

Bersham (North Wales) Women's Support Group
South Wales Coalfield Archive

Onllwyn Miners' Welfare Hall food distribution centre
Kay Bowen, co-ordinator, fourth from right
Photo by Hywel Francis

Point of Ayr Women's Support Group (North Wales)
Photo by Thalia Campbell

North Wales Congress 'occupation' of the constituency surgery of
Conservative Welsh Office Minister, Sir Wyn Roberts (Conwy)
Photo by Dorothea Heath

Occupation of Cynheidre Colliery by local women's support groups
South Wales Evening Post

Autographed Flying Pickets programme,
Treorchy Wales Congress concert,
December 1984
South Wales Coalfield Archive

Striking Miners' Christmas
fundraising concert at Hornsey,
6th December, 1984
South Wales Coalfield Archive

Y FANER

Baner ac Amserau Cymru

'A Strike-breaker is a traitor'

'Blacklegs' yng Nghwm Garw, De Cymru ym 1929

"Unodd brwydr y glowyr y Cymry, boed ffermwyr, lowyr neu athrawon, boed wragedd neu'r diwaith ... yn Gymry Cymraeg a di-Gymraeg, mewn ffordd na ddigwyddodd ers tro byd."

(Hywel Francis tud 14, 15)

Sefydlwyd 1843   DYDD GWENER, GORFFENNAF 20, 1984

Y Faner article by Hywel Francis in support of the strike, July 1984
Y Faner

Blaenant Colliery community picket, September 1984
Photo by Hywel Francis

Port Talbot march in support of strike
Tondu Photo Workshop

Maesteg Cymanfa Ganu,
5th September, 1984
South Wales
Coalfield Archive

Emlyn Williams, South Wales Area
President at time of sequestration,
outside NUM offices, Pontypridd,
1st August, 1984
South Wales
Coalfield Archive

Women's Support Group protest against benefit cuts,
Welsh Office, Cardiff, 30th July, 1984
Martin Shakeshaft – www.strike84.co.uk

Tower miners (including Tyrone O'Sullivan, top left) secure NUM offices against bailiffs at the time of sequestration, 1st August, 1984
Martin Shakeshaft – www.strike84.co.uk

*Early morning pickets at
South Celynen Colliery,
Newbridge, Gwent,
6th November, 1984*
*Martin Shakeshaft –
www.strike84.co.uk*

*Young supporters in commemorative Chartist Rally, Newport,
18th August, 1984*
Martin Shakeshaft – www.strike84.co.uk

Police action against NUM pickets, Orgreave Coke Depot, Yorkshire,
16th June, 1984
Martin Shakeshaft – www.strike84.co.uk

Maerdy (Rhondda Fach) Miners Institute food distribution, February 1985
Martin Shakeshaft – www.strike84.co.uk

By then the consensus in the coalfield, which had held the strike together for so long, was beginning to fracture. A local back-to-work movement, centred on Cynheidre in the far west, had been meeting secretly in London and South Wales, laying its plans, since August. Perhaps what was most remarkable was that, despite considerable financial resources, as well as the collaboration of the NCB and the police, only nineteen men returned on 5th November, sixteen of whom were in Cynheidre. Even by early January, that figure had risen to only 119, 90% of whom were concentrated at Cynheidre, which was marginally less than before Christmas. It was also clear that many of the leaders of the return were socially isolated and had experienced considerable social difficulties in the past.

Nevertheless, the intensity of feeling at this time was encapsulated in probably the largest indoor rally of the strike, at the Afan Lido in Port Talbot on 13th November, 1984. It was a sometimes frenzied, almost evangelical, occasion. When Norman Willis, the general secretary of the TUC, began to attack 'picket-line violence', a noose appeared before him. The refusal of the chairman to intervene, and subsequent media distortion of the event, transformed a very bad joke into a macabre incident.

What the NUM leaders in South Wales feared most at this time was not a collapse of the strike, but a violent backlash from communities that had hitherto been so disciplined, and that were increasingly penned in by police and poverty. Harassment by some police of men, women and children taking coal from anywhere they could find it became a dominating feature of daily life. Finding fuel, often by means of organised 'picket' teams cutting large areas of neighbouring forest, was then as important as food distribution to the maintenance of family and community morale. It was in this tense atmosphere that an ominous exchange had taken place between Weekes and his cousin, the Labour MP for Merthyr and Rhymney, Ted Rowlands:

> Ted had rung me up... saying that his wife Janice had been down on the picket line... and it had been extremely unpleasant... And for one of the few times during the strike, I lost my temper... And I said 'I've not heard a bloody word from the Labour Party for the last six months, and now you're telling me... I've got to stop two men who demand to go to work... I'm not going to do it!' He said 'There's going to be trouble then.' I said it was up to the NUM... And that was it. I put the phone down on him. Within two days, Ted was right and David Wilkie was killed. Now that was a hard one for me to swallow... that was the worst, the lowest point in the strike....

The taxi driver David Wilkie was killed by a concrete block dropped from a bridge as he drove a scab to work at Merthyr Vale Colliery on the morning of 30th November. His death was described by one Welsh church leader as the '... blackest day of the strike... The real culprits were those who were prepared to see the dispute go on and accept unnecessary casualties.' What made Merthyr Vale such a flashpoint was its location on the doorstep of historic Aberfan, scene of the 1966 disaster, in the midst of the most solid district in the British coalfield, the central valleys of South Wales. Compounding the problem were the police roadblocks, which prevented Merthyr Vale miners from travelling to their own colliery to picket. Nevertheless, the death of the young taxi driver, the immediate appearance of Margaret Thatcher on television to condemn the 'murder' and the subsequent arrest of three young miners (two of whom were later to stand trial for murder) did little to weaken the strike in South Wales, simply because it was such an aberration. It did, however, have a calming effect on the coalfield, best symbolised the following morning by Bill King, the veteran Merthyr Vale Lodge secretary. A young miner recalled the scene on the picket line:

> ... we stood in the pouring rain, Bill King asked ... for two minutes silence for everyone that had died as a result of the strike that was forced upon us. And we stood there [police and pickets], rain dripping off our noses, stunned virtually. But still Williams [the scab] came back to work ... in the convoy.

The women's groups then became even more prominent, as they stiffened picket line resistance – sometimes in the face of the hostility of the men. They also engaged in novel and imaginative forms of struggle, as at Cynheidre where they occupied the pit-head baths or in the Swansea valley where they sang hymns outside scabs' houses. By early December, however, the main preoccupation within all South Wales mining communities and amongst their supporters elsewhere was to get the best Christmas possible. The NUM in South Wales had pledged a turkey for every striking miner, a promise which created some bitter feelings in areas such as Gwent, where 'scrawny, 2-3 lb. chickens ... exacerbated problems' of morale. Herculean work was nevertheless undertaken by many organisations. For instance, the Hampshire support group raised £4,000 for toys and turkeys. The print unions, in particular, excelled themselves by adopting whole villages.

In the run–up to Christmas the press of the world seemed to descend on South Wales to visit this 'strange' coalfield that was uniquely solid. There was no doubt that a 'civilised' and 'decent' relationship existed between the employers, the union and the police, born partly out of past experiences. There is no doubt that 'problems' were 'sorted' quietly between local police and lodge officials in rugby clubs so as to avoid dividing communities. No-one asked what was happening – the watchword was always 'you only need to know what you need to know'.

That sense of commitment to 'community' extended to some of the members of the local media, notably Sarah Dickins of Gwent Community Radio and Aled Gwyn of BBC Radio Cymru. Aled was so 'close' to Welsh-speaking pickets, police tailed him to locate their next targets.

However, the new year brought old and new fears. An acceleration of the breakup of the strike elsewhere coincided with a growing realisation that there were to be no power cuts. In addition, twenty South Wales scabs were successful in obtaining a High Court order limiting the number of pickets permitted at each pit. Yet by 20th February, 1985, there were still only 478 men back at work, with the central valleys almost wholly unaffected. But the failure of talks – even with TUC, ACAS, church and NACODS' intervention – to achieve a just and fair settlement compounded a sense of profound isolation, which focused increasingly upon the potential consequences of the 'twelve month rule' (whereby individual strikers could be dismissed on the anniversary of the start of the dispute). For the South Wales leadership, as the days slipped by in 1985, their greatest worry became the very survival of the National Union itself.

From October 1984 onwards, the NUM Area leaders had toured the coalfield calling for continued loyalty. By the new year, it was loyalty alone that was sustaining the fragile unity of the committed activists and the majority of strikers, whose participation was limited to simply hanging on. At a Cynheidre general meeting, South Wales general secretary George Rees was faced with a cry of anguish that went to the very heart of the matter:

> I've lost my wife, my family, my house. Don't turn me into a scab.

When appeals for loyalty failed, union officials turned themselves into social workers and visited strike-breakers' homes. On one occasion:

> It was unbelievable. Shoes [were] burning in the fireplace.... The daughter was sitting there... her friend was having a birthday party and she had no clothes to go. ... There was hardly any food in the house at all.

In such circumstances, 'loyalty' took on a perverse new meaning. As the lodge chairman of Blaenant, Phil Bowen, began to say publicly, 'Does the last striker have the right to call the last but one a "scab"?' Throughout February there was a growing sense of isolation and vulnerability. Scabs were being encouraged by the NCB to form alternative lodge committees; and in one case, at St John's, leading lodge officials were dismissed by the NCB in circumstances that looked suspiciously like a set-up. The prospect of the re-emergence of a scab union had a particularly haunting meaning to many of the older lodge leaders, who had been nurtured on the primacy of unity and what veteran Dannie Canniff of Oakdale called 'the great democratic traditions of our union'.

The initiatives of colliery managers became more co-ordinated and emboldened into the new year. One such manager noted in his diary:

205 men telephoned 7-8 Feb. Notes also delivered by hand to remainder – delivered by undermanagers, engineers and surveyors... visited 15 men at home. 45 made contact....

At the same time, community pickets were mobilised and leaders of the Wales Congress sought, but failed, to have meetings with colliery managers at Abernant, Blaenant and elsewhere to ascertain the moral basis of their tactics of 'dividing communities'.

After the final breakdown of negotiations on the question of a written undertaking on 'uneconomic' pits, the South Wales leadership felt a great sense of anger when the National Executive failed on 28th February to give any recommendation other than 'stand firm'. What worsened the situation even further was the 'loyalty' to this latter position of right-wing National Executive members, who represented only handfuls of strikers. As George Rees acidly commented later, 'They were prepared to fight to the last drop of South Wales blood.' Beyond this, the public statements by the national president, Arthur Scargill, to the effect that Areas such as South Wales, where talk of a return to work without an agreement was gathering support, could use rule 41 to take unilateral action, merely compounded the problem. He appeared to be denying that the strike was a national one at all and to abnegate the responsibilities of the national leadership to provide a decisive and realistic lead. The South Wales leadership felt obliged to move rapidly into the strategic vacuum.

On St David's Day, 1st March, 1985, the South Wales Area Conference took the momentous decision, by an overwhelming majority, to call for a national return to work without an agreement. Motivated entirely by the need to save the National Union, Area President Emlyn Williams emphasised what the national leadership would not do: '... the vital necessity not merely to come out on strike under leadership, but also to go back under leadership.' It was not the time for leaders 'to hide in the shadows'. The week had witnessed a significant return to work, rising to over 5% in South Wales, but approaching 50% nationally. Some lodges only refused to support the unanimous EC motion because they had been mandated to stand by the six hundred miners who had been dismissed. It was a restrained and sober debate: many lodges knew that their pits were unlikely to survive the year. Six lodges were scab free to the end (the only ones in all the British coalfield) and eleven others had kept numbers down to single figures.

At the National Delegate Conference held at the TUC on Sunday, 3rd March, South Wales representative Des Dutfield deplored the National Executive's abrogation of its responsibility in not giving any recommendation. He accused them of looking for 'scapegoats' and for not having respect for those who had fought for twelve months. The Area vice president, Terry Thomas, was equally forthright in moving the ultimately successful 'return-to-work' motion. He called on delegates not to 'sit back with your blindfolds on and let the strike collapse around you. That is not leadership. I believe it is leadership if you are men enough to decide that the time is right when you have to make a strategic withdrawal....'

Amongst the NUM activists and their supporters there was a tension in the last days of the conflict between those who saw the need to preserve the National Union, to fight another day, and those who felt they could not return without their sacked comrades.

The notion of a hard core of 40% who would fight on forever was seen overwhelmingly in South Wales, and ultimately by the national conference, as a recipe for the destruction of the

NUM. Despite the bitter, chaotic scenes outside Congress House when the decision to return to work was announced and when South Wales delegates were harassed by an assortment of protesters, there was a tremendous – although by no means universal – sense of release in the valleys: not only was the strike over, but also there was the prospect of securing the future of the National Union. South Wales Area President Emlyn Williams had to be physically protected by Blaenant's Phil Bowen as long as they left the building.

These scenes were soon eclipsed in the popular memory by the drama of the return on the morning of Tuesday, 5th March. Much the most significant return for the immediate future of the coal mining communities of South Wales were the events at Cynheidre, where nearly 50% of the workforce by the end had broken with the strike. The young lodge chairman Tony Ciano stood on a chair in his colliery yard and shouted into the darkness:

I am delighted that over 800 of you [of a total NUM workforce of 1,100] marched in – united – behind the lodge banner this morning. I am proud that you did this because although many of you went back to work in the last few weeks you were driven back through despair and suffering and not through any lack of loyalty to the union or its struggles. You are **not** scabs....

There were similar demonstrations of unity and solidarity across the South Wales coalfield, most memorably perhaps, at 'scab free' Maerdy, 'the last pit in the Rhondda', whose emotional return was beamed by television companies across the world. Supporters from as far afield as Aberystwyth, Birmingham (with the TGWU Sandwell banner) and Oxford (with the Trades Council banner) heard defiant speeches from lodge chairman Arfon Evans and local women's support group leader Glynis Evans.

At Aberpergwm Colliery in the Neath Valley the diary of the colliery manager, Cliff Jones, spoke volumes:

STRIKE IS OVER. The pickets on the gate this morning were a miners' support group from Hampshire which included women. They cheered and sang the men back to work. The men marched in in order at about 6.25 am.

I met the dayshift in the canteen and welcomed them back to work.... Hwyl was excellent.

But the 'hwyl' did not last for long. Financial and mental exhaustion of the returning miners and their families – and the fear of loss of 'dole' in 1986 because of lack of contributions in 1984–85 – meant that NUM members unilaterally voted for closure before the end of the year. And that was invariably to be the experience elsewhere in the months and years ahead.

The NUM Fights for Wales:

The Birth of the Wales Congress

> Wales owes the miners everything: every national institution
> today has been built on their sweat and sacrifice.

These were the words of Deian Hopkin speaking at a rally held
at the 1984 Lampeter National Eisteddfod. His statement fixed
a mood, if not yet a movement, that was emerging across our
country. It was a new national dimension to the struggle which
was powerfully captured later in the slogan 'The NUM fights
for Wales'.

The industrial crisis in the South Wales valleys had created
the conditions in which there was the prospect for the
possibility of a wider mobilisation. It was building upon the
very special regard for the South Wales miners in every part of
Wales.

Twenty-five years after the miners' strike it can be suggested
that it was a defining moment in modern Welsh history. The
presiding officer at the National Assembly for Wales, Dafydd
Elis-Thomas, said at the 'Evolution of Devolution' conference on

6th November, 2008, 'that was when it all really began'. It was evident for sure that class and nationality converged on the National Eisteddfod field in Lampeter, and this achieved some degree of permanence with the creation of the Wales Congress in Support of Mining Communities in October 1984. The journey from there to the National Assembly in 1999 was a long, tortuous and some would say a tenuous one.

The British Miners' Strike of 1984–85 undoubtedly raised some fundamental questions concerning the nature of industrial and political alliances, particularly in Wales.

The NUM's fight for jobs, pits and communities in South Wales had been remarkable: after ten months barely 1% had broken the strike, and in the fourteen central valleys only fourteen had returned to work by mid January. The South Wales coalfield with over 20,000 miners had remained solid. Its experiences offered some useful lessons beyond the NUM and beyond the strike.

By contrast, however, support in the small North Wales coalfield (only two pits and less than two thousand men) was always patchy and virtually collapsed overnight in November.

The emergence in Wales of a broad democratic alliance of possibly a new kind – an anti-Thatcher alliance – was not the reason for this resistance. But an examination of its origins and development will perhaps begin to explain the intensity of the phenomenon. The Wales Congress in Support of Mining Communities grew out of a linked realisation that in order to feed miners' families more efficiently and in order to explain the case for coal more effectively, greater unity was needed. But what was also important was that it was a political realisation, born out of necessity within the miners' struggle, and arrived at virtually simultaneously by several political, trade union, cultural and other organisations.

When the Wales Congress in Support of Mining Communities was launched in Cardiff's City Hall on 21st October to consolidate and broaden support for the NUM's strike throughout Wales, its proceedings were dramatically interrupted by sixty London local government workers marching in with a banner proclaiming 'Brent Nalgo supports the Dulais Valley'.

The following week a large contingent of gays and lesbians were in the Dulais Valley as guests of miners' families because of their outstanding fundraising for the miners' cause. A short time later food arrived in West Wales from the Greenham Common women who had earlier in the strike been entertained by a South Wales striking miners' choir. In the weeks to come the Congress was involved in organising solidarity rallies in Cardiff, Pontyberem, Newbridge, Neath, Aberystwyth, Mountain Ash and Treorchy.

Even earlier in the year the sedate calm of respectable Wales, absorbing its annual dose of culture at the National Eisteddfod, was broken by public meetings on the Eisteddfod field in support of the miners. Farmers, church leaders, teachers, public employees, Welsh language activists, historians, poets, folk singers, communists, members of the Labour Party and Plaid Cymru, ministers of religion, the women's movement and the peace movement all made common cause in support of Welsh mining communities.

Out of this remarkable and new unity on the Eisteddfod field and a myriad of other new alliances elsewhere grew the Wales Congress.

Such seemingly unlikely and unexpected alliances could never have been anticipated by Nicholas Ridley, MP, when he drew up his secret anti-union and anti-strike plans in 1978, which anticipated major industrial strikes but did not foresee broad popular support for such struggles.

What was the political significance of these new alliances

forged during the miners' strike across and beyond the British coalfields and did the Wales Congress, in particular, represent a 'new politics'? Or would it all fade away with the end of this 'exceptional' industrial struggle?

Throughout the late summer of 1984 the NUM leadership was understandably preparing to maximise its support at the TUC and Labour Party Conferences in the autumn. But the real business of struggle and survival was going on elsewhere. For one reason or another, and with the benefit of hindsight, in a perverse way Eric Hammond of the electrician's union (the EEPTU) was right: the trade union movement, with the glorious exception of the railway workers, had not delivered the goods when and where it mattered. This is not to say that there had not been magnificent collections and tremendous public demonstrations. But Christmas parties and food parcels alone, important as they were, did not win majority public support, let alone achieve power cuts. The unpalatable truth was that the denial of a ballot divided the miners themselves, also divided them from the leadership of the TUC and the Labour Party, and crucially, via the national press, divided them from public opinion.

Old-fashioned trade union solidarity had, at best, been reduced to presentation turkeys at Christmas. At its worst, it was the army of well-paid faceless scab lorry drivers trundling daily along the M4 to supply foreign coke to Llanwern steelworks. That was the reality of an industrial battle that relied essentially on what amounted to no more than a 'syndicalist' strategy of industrial confrontation and regular sectional calls for a general strike and mass picketing to resolve the situation. But, the miners' strike at grass-roots level in every coalfield had been far more than that – it had to be because of the inadequacy of the Triple Alliance of railway workers, miners and steelworkers, and the inability of the TUC in enforcing its Congress decisions.

Nevertheless there was no doubt that the miners' struggle had often been conducted as if we were living in those far-off days of industrial militancy in the early 1970s – successful mass and flying pickets, workers' occupations and unemployment at less than a million. It was the era of unity of transport workers and miners on picket lines which gave birth to the Wales TUC. One other factor is forgotten about that period. Even though the two strikes of 1972 and 1974 were of relatively short duration, the victories were not achieved by industrial action and industrial solidarity alone. Despite power cuts, the miners won broad public support on the back of their just cause and their democratic ballot vote: this public support ultimately led to the fall of the Heath Conservative Government. There was broad support even if it did not develop into tangible broad alliances.

Since then the trade union movement had been debilitated by mass unemployment, impotent TUC leadership, the Thatcherite Conservative ideological offensive and successive state assaults on its very existence from Grunwick through to the NGA. Until the present miners' strike, the movement had been in retreat for years.

That survival, that resistance, was encapsulated in the words of an old Cynon Valley miner: 'After the experience of the last ten months, the miners and their communities have learnt how to survive together – they shouldn't ever have to fear the prospect of unemployment again.'

Even more perceptive and revealing was the simple ceremony in Italy during the strike when women activists from Coelbren and Hirwaun were made honorary members of the Italian resistance. In a period when the NUM was being attacked by every arm of the state, it was not an exaggeration to say that the union was being driven underground; the freezing of South Wales miners' funds through sequestration in

August was part of this process. The subsequent survival of the union in South Wales inevitably raised certain questions about its successful community and all-Wales strategies.

In this Welsh context, the nearest historical comparison we can make with the events of 1984–85 within communities and valleys is the broad unity and resistance during the miners' lockout of 1926 and in the mid-1930s on the questions of struggle over mass unemployment, scab unionism and aid for Republican Spain. At that time, class and community converged, significantly enough at a time of trade union weakness. Mining communities were becoming or had become unemployed communities and their struggles even embraced chapels and shopkeepers. Such struggles were essentially extra-parliamentary in character and involved the mobilisation of whole communities.

But that unity was transient and despite the courage of exceptional Labour leaders like Aneurin Bevan the broad-based unity around the South Wales Council of Action of 1935–36 was broken by the anti-communism of right-wing trade union and Labour leaders who saw Labourism as the rightful monolith in the valleys.

Nevertheless there were historical links. The strong sense of solidarity and the organic relationship between union, community and pit were still so intense that they could not be dismissed simply as blind loyalty to be 'lauded by future trade union historians' as South Wales Area Director Philip Weekes remarked when the anticipated return to work in South Wales again failed to materialise in the new year.

However, it would be much more fruitful for our purposes to examine our immediate past in order to understand the developments which led up to the Wales Congress.

There was no doubt that in many respects the Wales Congress might be seen as only a formalisation of what might have existed to an extent in all the other striking British coalfields, the most significant feature of which was the creation (as in 1926 but much more successfully – partly because there were fewer miners) of an alternative welfare system. Put more sharply it was a resistance movement. The way striking mining communities had responded to the threat to their very existence had been the most remarkable feature of the strike.

This socio-political development was undoubtedly part of the same phenomenon that resisted rate-capping in local government and opposed the abolition of the Greater London Council (GLC) and other metropolitan bodies, the mobilising of the unemployed around the People's March for Job and the mass peace campaigns against Cruise and Trident. In that sense they were all extra-parliamentary struggles that placed greater emphasis than hitherto on educating and mobilising communities and organisations in broad alliances.

In a Welsh context, there was a real difference in the kind of campaigning and the nature of alliances in the early 1980s: there was the women's anti-nuclear march from Cardiff to Greenham Common; Cymdeithas Yr Iaith Gymraeg (the Welsh Language Society) using an old slogan attributed to Caernarfon Labour MP Goronwy Roberts, 'heb gwaith dim iaith' (without work there is no language); valley parents involving themselves in direct action to oppose cuts in school bus services (including the setting up of an alternative school); and valley communities uniting with NUPE members to oppose hospital closures.

Intriguingly, Ffred Ffrancis, a leading member of Cymdeithas Yr Iaith, had proposed in the early stages of the development of the Wales Congress a much broader based alliance 'Cynulliad Cymreig: Amddiffyn Bywyd Cymunedol a Democratiaeth' ('Welsh Assembly to Defend Community Life and Democracy').

The common threads in all these struggles were the tactic of non-violent civil disobedience; the mobilising of people beyond the traditional parameters of the labour movement; and most important of all, the mobilising of whole communities in their own defence which crucially became a 'national' defence, and so emerged the slogan 'the NUM fights for Wales'.

What the McGregor NCB closures announcement in March 1984 did was to accelerate these trends and ultimately force their convergence on an all-Wales basis. To say that the Women Against Pit Closures' movement suddenly transformed women's attitudes is to misunderstand the processes which had already been operating in mining communities. The Greenham Common protest was started by working-class women in the Rhondda. Very many of the women active in the 1984–85 struggle were already prominently involved in politics and the peace movement at a local level.

Furthermore, Cymdeithas Yr Iaith Gymraeg had already made the link with workers in struggle well before the miners' strike. People and organisations were therefore already making connections: they were already identifying allies and enemies.

What the miners' strike in all the coalfields did was to begin to bring such developments together, involving not just single communities or groups of activities but whole regions and tens of thousands of people. It was also something beyond that. This new kind of alternative welfare system has created in many places a very resilient and tough resistance movement.

The network of women and mixed support groups had given rise to an alternative, community-based system of food, clothing, financial and morale distribution which has sustained about half a million people for nearly a year. The social and political skills of organisation and communication were akin to the experiences of people during a social revolution. Women, men and indeed children had learnt more about the strengths and weaknesses of the state apparatus, more about the problems of building working-class solidarity and above all more about their own individual and collective human potential than at any time in their lives. The new links within and between coalfields, with non-mining areas in Britain and indeed internationally were all pregnant with political possibilities. But increasingly that was a minority experience.

What emerged, nevertheless, was a network of unexpected alliances that went far beyond the traditional labour movement. It was a broad democratic alliance of a new kind – an anti-Thatcher alliance – in which the organised working class had a central role but a role which henceforth it would have to earn and not assume.

In this potentially permanent anti-Thatcher alliance, the women's movement and the peace movement had some transient prominence because, unlike the bulk of the trade union and labour movement during the run-up to the miners' strike, they played a crucial role in raising the political consciousness of the British people. Churches had a part in such an alliance because they raised very pertinent political, social and moral questions during the strike concerning the nature and role of the state and of the dehumanising character of capitalism. In particular, the initiative of the Welsh Council of Churches revealed a very deep under-standing of the political origins of the crisis facing all mining regions and put forward proposals to solve them, which placed the struggle in the wider context of government energy policy, what they have termed the 'vagaries of an undisciplined free market system' and the need to emphasise the dignity of human beings and communities.

Conscious of the human and organisational forces being unleashed by and for the miners in the midst of the crisis, the

Wales Congress in Support of Mining Communities initially set out to bring the debate back to one over the future of the coal industry rather than 'picket line violence' and to increase the unity around the mining communities. It was in effect an all-Wales support group.

What distinguished then the struggle in Wales, built as it was on the solid internal unity of the NUM in the South Wales coalfield? It was of course based on the unique triangular relationship between lodge, community and industry. Then there was the strong relationship between the NUM, the Wales TUC and the Labour Party. Added to that were the unique roles of both the Communist Party and Plaid Cymru.

And then there were the wider 'national' cultural, religious, peace and gender dimensions represented by Cymdeithas Yr Iaith, the Welsh Council of Churches, CND Cymru, the women's movement in all its forms and the gay and lesbian solidarity groups.

The diversity and complexity of the networks, sometimes overlapping, defied comparison with any other part of the British coalfields.

The four leaders of the Welsh Council of Churches – John Morgans, Noel Davies, Douglas Bale and Gronw ap Islwyn – succeeded in building church, indeed multi-faith, unity – never witnessed before or since.

John Morgans, the Moderator of the United Reform Church in Wales, became a leading figure in the Wales Congress and from its platforms spoke of the need for compassion, social justice and reconciliation. He was often fond of quoting the approach of the African National Congress: 'There can be no peace without first achieving justice!'

He and his fellow church leaders made a unique contribution to the distinctiveness of the Welsh 'resistance'. His diaries, now published in his autobiography, *Journey of a Lifetime* (2008), recognised the special circumstances then prevailing in Wales. He was struck by the ease with which he was able to achieve a sense of reconciliation between management and union in South Wales, in stark contrast to the national scene. He quoted *Sunday Times* journalist Donald McIntyre, who reported, 'The most significant development politically, not matched in any other coalfield, is a Wales Congress. It includes senior churchmen' (p. 371).

John Morgans was acutely aware when interviewed by Michael Crick of Channel 4 of the different perceptions of South Wales:

> Michael Crick had spent most of his time in Yorkshire researching his book [on Arthur Scargill]. He stated how he felt it was a totally different atmosphere in South Wales. There was a sense of community solidarity and a more reasoned and questioning attitude towards the dispute. There was no blind following of any leader and being swayed by demagogues. He wondered whether this was the result of the Welsh heritage. (p. 377)

The momentum in Wales for the 'Church Initiative', despite support from the NUM National Executive, the Labour Party leadership and the British Council of Churches, failed because the Conservative Government saw no advantage in a 'reconciliation' and gambled everything on a crumbling strike.

The Congress programme of aims, however, persisted in Wales and highlighted the need to identify and communicate the real issues at stake – the need for a sane energy policy and the safeguarding of jobs, communities, peace and democratic rights. It also sought to encourage local authorities to commission social audits of the effects of the current pit closure programme in their localities.

At a time when enormous pressures were building up on the NUM in South Wales, particularly as a result of sequestration and fundraising, the Congress sought to get the Welsh people to carry their share of the burden.

Indeed the Congress very quickly received backing from over three hundred prominent people in Welsh politics (Plaid, Labour and CP), local government, trade unions, the churches, the arts, farmers, the women's movement and the peace movement. Very significantly Neil Kinnock, the then leader of the Labour Party who was being criticised for calling for a miners' ballot, became a supporter. This commitment and his support of the 'Church Initiative' helped heal a breach with the struggle at grass-roots level as many of his constituents were on strike.

The Congress was born out of a realisation by large sections of the Welsh people that the miners were struggling for the future of Wales. If Thatcherism could defeat the miners, then all Welsh communities were in danger. Its steering committee embraced all these organisations and met weekly to discuss strategy. There were remarkably few differences over tactics or political initiatives although its chair frequently argued privately with Kim Howells over his high media profile, despite not being an elected NUM official.

The miners' strike had therefore created a Welsh unity and identity, overcoming language and geographical differences, which failed to materialise in 1979 during the referendum when a four-to-one vote rejected devolution. It was the fear of such a return to the superficial and sterile politics of devolution of 1979 that made a tiny number within the Welsh labour movement hesitate about associating with the Congress. Significantly, their influence was negligible. Dark hints of a 'Commie and Nats plot' was the language of the past. They soon realised that unless they joined, the world would pass them by.

Indeed the growing unity within Wales was to an extent replicated in Westminster where Plaid's Dafydd Elis-Thomas spoke frequently in support of the NUM and an Early Day Motion by Labour's Ann Clwyd, Denzil Davies and Alun Williams received the support of the Liberal MP Geraint Howells.

One of the great advantages of the Wales Congress was that it ensured that the NUM never felt isolated within Wales. Just as the Wales Congress was launching a series of nationwide rallies in November, the NCB in South Wales started to increase its aggressive managerial onslaught on the still rock-solid NUM membership. Congress leaders including Labour Euro-MP David Morris and Plaid President Dafydd Elis-Thomas, MP, and Cynon Valley Labour MP Ann Clwyd spearheaded a counterattack by attempting to interview NCB managers personally. They wished to ask why were they, as trade unionists, prepared to supervise scabs (unlike NACODS) and why were they actively participating in a government plan that would ultimately socially divide and industrially destroy mining communities.

The solidarity of the miners in South Wales held, and the Congress played its part then and later in holding the line to 1% despite over a year of struggle.

After less than two months the Congress was already strengthening itself by decentralisation. Local Congresses appeared in North Wales and the Rhondda, and there was the prospect of others in all the valleys, in Cardiff, London, Ireland and even Nottingham. London did materialise with a launch in the last week of the strike, with a conference at the GLC addressed by Ken Livingstone, and a concert with Elvis Costello, Billy Bragg, The Men They Couldn't Hang and the South Wales Striking Miners' Choir, which raised £5,000.

The strike in Wales had therefore not just been about mass picketing. It had been about how people began to take control of their own lives. It had been about women and men from all the coalfields learning about the many-sided role of the state in industrial battles and that the fight for jobs and communities was and is the experience elsewhere in Britain and abroad. When the South Wales Striking Miners' Choir entertained an entirely black audience in Walsall, one of the choristers paid tribute to the 'ethnic minorities' that had been so outstanding in their support during the strike. A black leader responded: 'The Welsh are the ethnic minority in Walsall.'

The Wales Congress tried to build an anti-Thatcher democratic alliance that would hopefully have gone beyond the strike and turn all those so-called 'minorities' who had supported them into an irresistible and united majority to fight for peace, jobs and communities. It was anticipated that there would inevitably be problems, the greatest of which would be the possibility that all the positive features of unity and experience everywhere could be eclipsed by the fragmentation of the NUM. And that is what happened, and we need only to look at the fate of the North Wales coalfield to begin to understand how fragile unity was in the NUM.

South Wales pickets had arrived in the North Wales coalfield very early in the strike and succeeded in stopping Bersham Colliery but they soon realised that appeals to solidarity or even to a common nationhood were not to be long-lasting. Ali Thomas however returned to the Dulais Valley saying, 'They're not Welsh miners, they're Liverpool car workers!'

In retrospect it can be said that the fragmentation of the strike in North Wales mirrored more closely the pattern across the British coalfields; in that sense South Wales was the aberration not North Wales.

North Wales had historically always been a moderate coalfield. By 1984 the two remaining pits, Point of Ayr on the coast drawing its workforce in part from Lancashire and Bersham, from the older mining communities surrounding Wrexham, were led by Area Secretary Ted McKay who tended to side with the minority right wing on the NUM NEC.

Encouraged by South Wales pickets, Bersham was solidly on strike by the end of April, and this influenced a sizable minority at Point of Ayr who also struck. But the strike was eroded by some working miners taking legal action.

Liverpool proved crucial to strikers at both collieries. Historian David Howell in his excellent account of the strike in the coalfield wrote of the 'bleak experiences' collecting in seaside communities in contrast to the more solid support from the quarrying district of Blaenau Ffestiniog. A member of the Point of Ayr's women's support group also spoke at the 1984 Plaid Conference. The two pits had women's groups who were involved in picketing, public speaking and fundraising, some afar afield as France.

But the early divisions remained and were exacerbated by lack of coherent mining communities, unlike in South Wales.

With the big national push for a return to work in November, the strike eventually collapsed in both pits although small numbers did remain to the end.

Divisions during the strike manifested themselves in the aftermath with the emergence, albeit briefly, of the Union of Democratic Mineworkers (UDM) in both pits. The failure to persuade the Area's leaders to join the UDM and the appeals for national unity to preserve the two remaining pits meant that the coalfield ultimately remained loyal to the end of coal mining in North Wales.

North Wales played little part in the wider political discussions in Wales, then or later, which prefigured the narrowly successful 'Yes campaign' for democratic devolution in 1997. Indeed the poor 'Yes' vote in North East Wales mirrored that lack of a radical outlook so evident in 1984–85.

Kim Howells wrote at the time that the intensity of the struggle in South Wales required the creation of 'new defences' and the rediscovery of 'old socialist and collectivist truths' in overcoming 'the worst that the state apparatus could throw at them'.

He summed it up in this way, prophetically hoping for future democratic advances:

> In South Wales we also discovered something else: that we are part of a real nation which extends northwards beyond the coalfield, into the mountains of Powys, Dyfed and Gwynedd. For the first time since the industrial revolution in Wales, the two halves of the nation came together in mutual support. Pickets from the south travelled to the nuclear and hydro-stations in the north. Support groups in the north brought food, money and clothes to the south. Friendships and alliances flourished; old differences of attitude and accent withered and out of it grew the most important 'formal' political organisation to emerge during the course of the strike – the Wales Congress in Support of Mining Communities.

Those sentiments were echoed by Angharad Tomos, political education officer of Cymdeithas Yr Iaith, in a letter to the Wales Congress Chairman, on 7th November, 1984:

> Credaf fod mawr angen meithrin perthynas mwy clos rhwng tueddiadau radicalaidd yn y gogledd a'r de. Mae'r streic wedi bod yn gyfnod i bontio gagendor fel mae 'Radical Wales' a symudiadau diweddar eraill wedi ei wneud.

(I believe there is a great need to nurture a closer relationship between the radical tendencies in the north and the south. The strike has been a period of bridging the gulf as 'Radical Wales' has done with other recent movements.)

Such was the momentum provided by the enthusiasm from the Wales Congress that it was decided to relaunch it at a major conference at Maesteg on 1st June, partially funded by a generous donation from playwright Karl Francis. Maesteg was chosen because of the threatened closure of local colliery St John's Colliery.

The commitment of the conference delegates was to work with the NUM to argue the case for coal; defend pits, jobs and communities; fight against victimisation; campaign on behalf of jailed miners; and alleviate continuing hardship. The Wales TUC, the Labour Party, Plaid Cymru and the Communist Party all endorsed the Congress' continued existence.

An exhibition produced by Tondu Photo Workshop's Gary Bevan and Hazel Gillings (who tragically died shortly afterwards) toured Wales and Ireland telling the story of the strike. Notably it visited the Rhyl National Eisteddfod of 1985 where Sian James and I spoke at a rally and at a concert organised by Cymdeithas Yr Iaith.

That occasion, in North Wales, surrounded by fresh memories of new alliances and new solidarity, was evocative of a kind of another national defeat, prefigured in Idris Davies' epic poem of 1926, which was, after all, deliberately called *Gwalia Deserta*.

As collieries closed at an increasing pace and struggles emerged elsewhere, support groups faded and so did the Wales Congress which did not survive beyond 1986. But some would claim that the legacy of unity and of struggle survived well into the following decade.

That was certainly the view of John Morgans, the leading moral force behind the 'Church Initiative' and a major influence in the Wales Congress. His thoughts were clear and unequivocal, faithfully recorded in his diary at the time, highlighting as it did the need for future allies:

This is a bitter blow for all who have struggled and sacrificed for a year, but there can be no compromise with the ruthless Thatcherite view of society. The Church must identify itself with a view of a just and compassionate society, and discover allies in the long struggle ahead. (p. 378)

The Experience of Defeat:

1985–92

On the dole, it's a lonely place... you don't talk about being poor if you are poor because you've got so much pride... I was going up the old pit for a walk the other day and this woman was coming down with an empty flask... She said 'I've just been taking him a cup of tea.' I thought 'What the hell has she been taking him a cup of tea for?' It then occurred to me that he was picking coal and had been for four years. I forgot the woman's husband – and I'm supposed to be sensitive to people – she'd been taking him a flask of tea. And she said 'It's a lonely place up there.'

Barbara Walters,
Afan Valley women's support group,
27th November, 1985

Was this the story of the South Wales valleys after the strike? As the months slipped by, the year-long strike became ever more a brave, honourable interlude; a breathing space for communities that had always known hardship, and a strike, however long, was for them ironically a necessary talisman against the obscenities of a miner's life. The Rhondda novelist Gwyn Thomas described 'the life of a miner, as a whole, [as] a kind of outrage and all the cosmetic increases in conditions and pay will not alter that ... it is fundamentally an anomaly under the sun that men should leave the sun and work in these dark and dangerous places' (quoted in John Ormond's BBC Wales television series 'The Colliers' Crusade', 1980).

Colliery closures in South Wales had invariably, in earlier times, been 'accepted'. But the 1980s were different. In the 1960s there was always somewhere else – another pit, another factory, another town. Even those mining villages and even whole valleys which lost their pits somehow hung on and survived. What was then experienced was the disappearance of coal mining, the disappearance of work – and skilled work – from large parts of South Wales.

But it was the speed of the closures, like a whirlwind scattering fragile communities, that was so stunning and new. Ten pits in six months closed for the most part, in the end, by family debts, by fear not of an uncertain future but of no future at all, and by perhaps most of all a desire to get out.

On the weekend the strike was being called off, the talk in the miners' welfares was of 'the strike ending, but the struggle goes on'. A mixture of relief, elation, anxious anticipation and controlled anger characterised discussions in strike committees and support groups alike. At Onllwyn, the strike centre for three western valleys, where less than 1% had returned, there was strange, lurid, emotive language: 'it's difficult for a scab to crawl out of the pit without a leg or an arm'; 'you can starve by the leg of a mandrill or by the leg of a table'; 'plenty of cold water and walk slow'. Such remarks interspersed the more serious discussions on an amnesty for victimised miners, on continuing food parcels (which were provided there and elsewhere for at least another week) and maintaining new friendships and political links with those who had assisted in the struggle.

Encouraged by the South Wales Area leadership, many of the community and women's support groups stayed in existence to assist with the inevitable continuing hardship and the campaign to reinstate sacked and jailed miners. The Wales Congress and the South Wales Women Support Group also chose to keep going, and they were soon joined by the launching of the South Wales axis of the Coalfield Communities Campaign. The local, regional and national alliances were thus kept alive, at least for the time being; there was even a degree of optimism that the strike would bequeath a legacy of new forms of political organisation and mobilisation.

In the first days and weeks following the return, anger and bitterness against management were kept under control by lodge discipline and fear of victimisation. But the volatile feelings of the community were another matter. An attack on the wife of a 'super scab' whilst driving her car out of the Aberaman phurnacite plant indirectly precipitated the sacking of five leading activists, none of whom had apparently been involved in that or any other incident. Spontaneous sympathy strike action at neighbouring pits further exposed a deep-seated anger. That anger revealed itself again when guilty verdicts were passed on 17th May on the two Rhymney miners, Russell Shankland and Dean Hancock, accused of murdering David Wilkie, the Cardiff taxi driver. Large demonstrations in their support at Rhymney and Cardiff, instigated by the Rhymney Valley Support Group, were another indication of the continued commitment to the victims of the struggle, if not the struggle itself. The sentences were later reduced on appeal when the charges were successfully reduced to manslaughter.

However, the painful task of coming to terms with defeat had begun in South Wales immediately after the strike ended. There were some understandably emotional outbursts, such as the proposal at the South Wales NUM Executive Council – only defeated on the casting vote of Emlyn Williams – to withdraw the union from the Wales TUC because of a perceived failure to achieve sufficient solidarity. However, overwhelmingly, problems were confronted in a sober and pragmatic fashion. To save the union as a viable organisation, the Area leadership purged its contempt by apologising in the High Court and in so doing freed its sequestrated assets. On another front, it quietly began to negotiate – without a public campaign – on behalf of its sacked members and within two weeks their number had been reduced from seventy-eight to twelve. This was achieved through the relative strength of the union and the sympathetic approach of the Area NCB Director, whose expressed – albeit privately held – wish was to reinstate all possible sacked miners before his own retirement in June. This realism extended to those on trial for criminal damage and criminal conspiracy for the occupations of the South Wales steel plants. For their contrition in pleading guilty, they were sentenced to twelve months, bound over for two years.

This realism was but a reflection of the defeat which became the daily experience of men in the pits and their families in the communities. A heavy price was being exacted for endurance and loyalty: mental and physical exhaustion and a management able to ride roughshod over the workforce. Some managers took advantage. Long-established customs were abolished, such as the .early Friday finish at Aberpergwm, but this only served to embitter industrial relations and, in this case, helped hasten the end of the pit itself. Yet the low morale and isolationism never turned into hostility towards the NUM. The breakaway so-called Union of Democratic Mineworkers (UDM) failed to establish a bridgehead in South Wales. The tiny number who joined (no more than half a dozen) were soon won back. The disappearance of the 'super scabs' through early redundancy or transfers to other coalfields only served to underline the continued hegemony of the NUM in the pits. Characteristically, South Wales was the only coalfield where the UDM made no impact whatsoever.

Nevertheless, within ten months of the strike, nine collieries had disappeared in South Wales, five of them between 20th September and 7th October, 1985. With the exception of St John's, where there was some spirited local opposition focused upon an Independent Public Inquiry (assisted by Mid Glamorgan County Council), a mixture of bitterness, anger and resignation were the only real responses. After a year of magnificent collective resistance, individualistic solutions through the acceptance of redundancy became the pattern. Most of the closures were, however, expected: miners and their families had lived with threats of particular closures for years (Celynen South since 1970). Only Aberpergwm and Abertillery New Mine (Roseheyworth) took the NUM by surprise. There, and elsewhere, the fear of the loss of redundancy payments and unemployment benefits, as well as the burden of accumulated debts, helped precipitate the closures.

The year 1986 saw the further closures of Blaenserchan, Coedely and Abercynon as separate productive units. And in the autumn, these were followed by the closure of two former 'flagships' of the coalfield, Cwm and Nantgarw. By the end of the year, employment had been cut by nearly half, although, equally revealing, labour productivity had rocketed, through increased capital investment, new work practices and, most crucially, the elimination of less productive units.

Employment & Labour Productivity in South Wales Coalfield, October 1983 – October 1986

	Employment	Output per man shift (tons)
October 1983	21,500	7.17
October 1986	11,943	11.44

Source: NUM (South Wales Area)

The intensity of these losses, along with the closure of associated workshops and coke ovens, dealt body blows to the morale of the valley communities. At Garw in Mid Glamorgan, for example, only fifty out of a workforce of six hundred accepted transfer to other collieries. This response was characteristic:

> I'm sick and fed up with the Coal Board and their tactics. After thirty-four years ... I don't want to work for the Coal Board ever again and I'm glad my two boys have nothing to do with the Coal Board either.

South Wales had long suffered closures. What was new in 1985–86 was the final disappearance of coal mining from large parts of the valleys. From the river Neath in the west to the river Ely in the east, not a single pit survived on the southern rim of the coalfield. The valleys had not been so silent in a hundred years. During that winter there was a collective pessimism about the future; a gloom which was only partially lifted by the reduction of the life sentences on the 'Rhymney two' to eight years for manslaughter. This despair was felt all the more acutely in those valleys which had lost their own pits during the 1960s and which thus saw 1984–85 as truly a last stand. Activists in the Abergwynfi and Glyncorrwg women's support groups in just such a valley (the Afan) felt isolated and highly vulnerable when St John's, the single remaining pit in the neighbouring valley, itself closed. Their feelings were apocalyptic. These were the feelings of Barbara Walters of Glyncorrwg:

> We all feel that we are on the edge really because they are very small villages up here really. They are all stable communities but they are just going beyond that. They are just viable at the moment... there are so many houses that are empty, they are going to fall down....
>
> What beginning is there of something new? Now we can see the end of an industry in these valleys... When we didn't have industry, a craftsman was able to come in and use his craft to help set up an industry, but I don't know where we are going.

In such remote communities, the closures of schools and libraries, the end of bus services, the demolition of houses, the loss of a doctor from a practice, even the disappearance of a telephone kiosk, were all cumulative symptoms of a long-term decline. But this last rundown of colliery closures severed the surviving link with an industry that had given birth to these communities barely a century before.

And yet a resilience, a community spirit and a political consciousness, stiffened by the recent struggle, remained. As workers and their families struggled elsewhere, the links of 1984–85 were invoked. Broadwater Farm, Wapping, Silent Night and the Blaenau Ffestiniog slate strikes, even faraway liberation movements in Nicaragua and South Africa, and London's Gay Pride commanded support from the support groups and the South Wales NUM alike.

Within the NUM, however, the tensions between the South

Wales Area and the national leadership, which derived from disagreements over the conduct and conclusion of the strike, did not resolve themselves with the passing of time. Differences were manifold and focused upon issues such as the potential for renewing the struggle through industrial action; the long delay in getting national funds released through the courts; the failure to resolve the wages issue; the emphasis upon a public campaign to reinstate sacked miners; and the centralisation of decision making, within the union, at the possible expense of local democracy. At root, however, these were symptoms of a much more fundamental divergence over the politics of the labour movement.

The South Wales leadership, in accepting the realities of defeat, sought new perspectives, new explanations, new alliances and a healing of old divisions. In his 1984–86 Report, Area General Secretary George Rees wrote:

> The Labour Movement must use this interregnum to rebuild its self-confidence and reassess its perspectives. Beneficial alliances and long-term policies are easier to construct and formulate when the demands for industrial conflict are more absent than present... If we do not seize the opportunity and fill the vacuum of strategic planning and sane forecasting on energy matters, rest assured that others hostile to our cause soon will.

These tensions and differences centred on the need to reunify the union. 'Anger is not enough,' Michael McGahey said in his 1986 NUM Annual Conference when calling for an approach to the UDM. But his call went unheeded, and the consequence was further decline in membership, influence and power, industrially and politically.

Meanwhile away from the valleys, what was the new political class ruling Wales thinking of the 1984–85 defeat, or for them, their victory? At a seminar in the late 1980s organised by the Institute of Welsh Affairs, one successful businessman suggested that the way to help 'solve our problems' was to rename the valleys 'Greater Cardiff'. It would have been a savage irony, for Cardiff would still be a sleepy fishing village but for what Gwyn Thomas called 'those great coal gulches to the north'.

This question of image was, however, a well-considered and challenging proposal: the miners' strike of 1984–85 was now thankfully part of harmless history, the pits were nearly all flattened or had become museums and the imminent arrival of the Cardiff Bay Development surely prefigured a 'Cymric-Japanised' Greater Boston. It could be the final nail in the coffin of that Welsh proletariat which had allegedly been 'fashioned' by the historians, sociologists and playwrights of the 1970s and 1980s.

The renaming, at a stroke, of the valleys was a serious proposition: as serious as renaming St Petersburg and then Leningrad, later. It was an affirmation of political power and a changing world. Words and names, as Raymond Williams would have gently reminded us, are weighty matters. And especially so with the valleys because they were synonymous with a particular kind of distinctive monoculture: coal, community, nonconformity (of many kinds), trade unionism, self-education, democracy and socialism. All this proletarianism did not fit comfortably into the world of the Conservative Government's 'Valleys Initiative': the enterprise culture was not a collectivist, communal culture. Could such a dramatic culture shift be achieved, in readiness for the next century, through the combination of the closure of an industry (and one which created that unique valleys community) and a simple change of name?

The painful process of transforming the valleys from a proletarian heartland into what could conceivably be called 'Greater Cardiff', in readiness for the twenty-first century, began in the 1980s. It was not simply a question of a major industry being slimmed down and then disappearing, it required an ideological shift away from a set of cultural values that had evolved over the previous century.

That ideological shift was away from what the Welsh 'Church Initiative' of 1984–85 represented, built as it was on the community ethos of the 'Call to the Valleys' following the Aberfan disaster of 1966. That popular and populist notion of empowerment reached deep into our history and was so resonant in the strike. The 'Call' was to

... invite the people to examine themselves, to rediscover what has made them what they are, to choose in a new age what they are going to be.

By contrast, this 'new age' for the new Conservative Secretary of State for Wales, Peter Walker (who as Energy Secretary had presided over the victory of the miners) was something rather different.

In June 1988, the Valleys Programme, more commonly known as the 'Valleys Initiative', was launched, with £500 million of public money generating a further £1,000 million in private money, which it was claimed would ensure that '... the next century will provide the area with new and diverse jobs and a better environment with fine amenities for sport and recreation, good housing and a rich cultural and community life'.

Although heralded as a rolling programme, it neither formulated a realistic short-term plan to answer major redundancies as at Oakdale and Merthyr Vale collieries and Hoover's in August

81

1988, nor a long-term Government-funded plan which addressed the serious socio-economic questions of long-term unemployment, poor housing and low-quality training and education. The Cardiff Business School's report, *Divided Wales* (1988), highlighted the widening gap between the wealthy areas of Clwyd, Gwent and the Vale of Glamorgan and the relative impoverishment of the central valleys. The report observed:

> Certainly the Government has recognised a problem area: it remains to be seen whether the 'Programme of the People' will work.... When considering any intra-regional differences within Wales, this should be placed in the context of a poorly performing region which has been slipping further behind the prosperous South of England and the revived Midlands ... this relative decline is illustrated by a number of social, economic and industrial indicators. This is in stark contrast to the picture portrayed by certain politicians and agencies.

Divided Wales scratched beneath the 'greening' overlay of coniferous forests, garden festivals, mining museums, heritage parks and nearby marinas, and revealed very grave problems. The worst example of deprivation was to be found in the Cynon Valley: it had only 0.39% professional people; 60% of its households had an income of less than £4,000; only 5.6% of households had an income of more than £12,000.

The Government's push toward an 'enterprise culture' was mirrored in the British Coal Enterprise strategy with its Job and Career Change Scheme (JACCS). There had been an unseemly haste on the part of British Coal to close pits rapidly, sometimes in a matter of days, as at Abernant and Blaenant. There was little concern for emotional matters, proper guidance and counselling or financial advice. JACCS was an attempted coherent strategy, but studies revealed that there were still serious gaps in quality training, educational opportunities and career guidance particularly for craftsmen with 'industry specific' skills and those who needed basic literacy and numeracy skills.

The Government's Valleys Programme, as a sin of omission, recognised only a post-coal era by mentioning the industry merely only as a part of history. It placed the 'enterprise culture' at the heart of the valleys' regeneration and transformation. But most academic observers were sceptical about its likely success. The imminence of the one European Market and energy privatisation, the NUM believed, would surely wipe out what was left of the South Wales coal industry by the mid-1990s. Lack of major central and local government spending, especially in high-quality training and education, coupled with the impact of the community charge and rising house process would only serve to further erode social cohesion in valley communities.

The Valleys Initiative merely masked the recognition by a Conservative Government of valleys without coal. In the words of Peter Walker in his 1991 autobiography *Staying Power*, it was 'to clean up the valleys and adopt a series of measures' (p. 207). It did not recognise the deep social and economic consequences following the destruction of the coal industry.

By 1992, the South Wales coalfield faced extinction. Conservative Government policies were moving swiftly towards coal privatisation and in any event the grand schemes for the valleys made no reference to a future with coal, unless there was a change of Government. The experience of defeat seemed to be unending.

Resourcing

A Journey of Hope:

1992-2009

1992 was a defining moment in the long decline of the NUM and the nationalised coal industry. The failure to return a Labour Government earlier in the year meant that coal privatisation was inevitable. There was a remarkable, yet brief, flourish of solidarity and indignation, an echo of 1984–85, when a massive London demonstration in September protested against a final round of pit closures which had been conceived by the Conservative Deputy Prime Minister, Michael Heseltine. But that was not the end of the story.

In the decade after the 1984–85 struggle, transferred skilled miners and craftsmen, all seasoned trade unionists, gathered at Tower for what was to be the inevitable last stand. Phil White from St John's in the Llynfi Valley, Dai 'Ropey' Davies from Penrhiwceiber in the Cynon Valley, Graham Taylor from Maerdy in the Rhondda Fach, Ken Williams from Lewis Merthyr in the Rhondda Fawr, Wayne Thomas from Abernant in the Swansea Valley and Dave Proctor from Durham joined such local veteran campaigners as Tyrone O'Sullivan and Glyn Roberts to enrich the local leadership with their diverse industrial, political and community experiences. Tower by the early 1990s became a microcosm of the whole South Wales coalfield drawing its workforce from Pontypool in the East to the Gwendraeth Valley in the West.

Despite the protests, the Government achieved its closures and ultimately the privatisation of the industry. Tower had been in the vanguard of the struggle in 1992, as in 1984–85. By April 1994 it was the last deep mine in South Wales. Under privatisation the workforce believed there was a conspiracy to close this profitable mine. In what became known as the 'Fourteen Days that Shook Britain' a public campaign across the country culminated in a march of 280 miles to London and a stay-in strike by local Labour MP Ann Clwyd and veteran Tower miner Glyn Roberts.

Thousands of letters and many donations were received in this period. The threat of closure was remarkably withdrawn, but ultimately British Coal forced the lodge to make the tactical retreat of accepting redundancy because new work practices resulted in drastic reduction in wages. But at no time did they accept the closure which ultimately came on the 23rd April.

The struggle moved on to preparing for the impossible dream of a workers' buyout. Cynon Valley Borough Council provided rent-free offices for the campaign, professional support came from the Wales Co-operative Centre and enormous public backing was received from all those who had benefited from Tower's solidarity in the past. Two million pounds was raised by the 239 miners who pledged £8,000 each from their redundancy payments to achieve the buyout.

The success of the Tower Employees Buyout (TEBO) in winning the tender in October 1994 and its subsequent successes in meeting productivity targets and winning new markets locally and overseas were very much in the spirit of the struggles of previous generations: the linking of eternal vigilance to economic freedom had come full circle.

On 23rd December, 1994, ownership of Tower Colliery passed from British Coal to Goitre Tower Anthracite Ltd, the new name under which TEBO would operate. On 2nd January, 1995, Tower miners, their families and many supporters marched back to the pit to take over its ownership. It was an inspiring and emotional occasion, full of political irony and paradox: the workers took control of Tower as the rest of the industry was privatised. As one old miner remarked, 'This is better than 1947. Then the Government became the owners but now it's the miners at last. Then they flew the Union Jack over Tower but now we are flying the red dragon of Wales....'

TEBO was led by the seemingly unlikely combination of Philip Weekes, former chairman of the National Coal Board in South Wales, and the Tower lodge secretary Tyrone O'Sullivan. These fellow socialists had found a 'third way', very much in the tradition and history of the pit, its community and much of Wales itself. Tower had become a beacon for others struggling for economic and community survival: its commitment to the policies of community enterprise and sustainable development was but a modern version of the valleys' collectivist community traditions. And its commitment to local cultural, sporting and charitable causes set an ethical example for other employers to follow. Its support in particular for the revival of the South Wales Miners' Eisteddfod had been a heartwarming initiative.

The closure of Tower in 2008 through the natural exhaustion of coal reserves after fourteen years of a profitable co-operative enterprise coincided with an upturn in coal demand worldwide. Tower miners were transferred to two local mines, Unity and

Pentreclwydau, in the Neath Valley. There is also the prospect of a new Corus/Tata drift mine at Margam whose plans under the late Philip Weekes had been abandoned in 1987.

Tower had survived privatisation and the near collapse of the industry to witness the possible rebirth of coal in South Wales at a time of renewed interest in public ownership under a Labour Government: history must, at last, be on our side!

The community and co-operative ethos of Tower was replicated in many initiatives across the South Wales valleys, often encouraged by the Wales Co-operative Centre, which had given vital financial guidance to Tower. In 1996, on the eve of the return of a Labour Government, the Valleys Initiative for Adult Education (VIAE) reviewed in *Chasing the Dragon* the range of community responses to the long crisis in the South Wales coalfield.

Some of these initiatives, such as the DOVE women's training co-operative at Banwen in the Dulais Valley, grew directly out of the experiences of 1984–85. The writer Raymond Williams referred to the resources of hope that we derived during that struggle – the common use and special meaning attached by striking miners and women supporters to such key words as 'community', 'culture', 'democracy' and 'co-operation'.

The election and re-election of Labour Governments since 1997 and the creation through democratic devolution of the National Assembly for Wales have begun to address the deep levels of social and economic deprivation caused by the collapse of the coal industry following the defeat in 1985. The establishment of the Coalfield Regeneration Trust, the securing of European Objective One Status for West Wales and the Valleys (and its successor Convergence Funding), the setting up of the first Social Justice Department by the Welsh Assembly Government and its location in Merthyr Tydfil and renewed government interest in clean coal technology have all been important policy initiatives in recent years.

There is a welcome emphasis by the Welsh Assembly Government on economic regeneration of valleys communities, centring initially on the Heads of the Valleys Programme in 2004, its Turning Heads strategy in 2006 and most recently its West Wales Valleys Strategy. But much greater public investment is needed and as Dr Victoria Winckler, Director of the Bevan Foundation, stated in 2008, very much in the spirit of the democratic impulses of 1984–85:

> ... the programme needs to engage more effectively with people within the heads of the valleys area. The programme must not be imposed from above – it needs to be owned, and have the belief of, the people whom it is supposed to serve.

Those two great institutions of postwar Britain, the nationalised coal industry and the NUM, no longer dominate our economic and political landscape, largely as a consequence of the intensity and length of the dispute.

After the strike, the writer Bea Campbell posed this perceptive question:

> In decades to come, when we come to write and reflect upon the history of this strike as a watershed in working class politics, the real test of change to come will be whether this women's movement is allowed to survive – for the women themselves.

Today, one of the small but growing number of young mining apprentices in the South Wales coalfield, Carwyn Donovan, employed at the Unity Mine, provides an essential link with the past. His parents, Carole and David, who met during this period, represent the finest traditions of solidarity between the coalfield and the wider world during 1984–85. Carwyn's commitment to his industry, his community and his union are vital clues to our understanding of our past, and our future.

Reflecting on the past quarter of a century, the experience of defeat has, in some ways, meant some seeking of new explanations and some new perspectives. The valleys are, after all, still with us. Despite everything, they have not become part of a 'Greater Cardiff'. There is a slowly reviving coal industry and we are certainly part of a much more democratic Wales, and their efforts helped achieve that. History then is on our side? Nevertheless the reality of economic and social loss, changing gender relationships and the enduring sense of community remain the lasting and conflicting legacies of the year-long struggle.

A Note on Sources

Much of this book is based upon my writings in the mid-1980s, almost but not entirely in the 'heat' of the struggle, and this sometimes shows in the sense of engagement and commitment in the language and style. I have tried to retain some of that intensity although my 'training' as an historian is hopefully sometimes evident and with the passing of time some more considered judgements are necessarily made.

Some of the primary source material of the period (minutes of support groups, union minutes, photographs, tapes, etc.) are located at the South Wales Miners' Library and the South Wales Coalfield Archive at Swansea University and at such public record offices as the West Glamorgan Archives Service.

BOOKS

Martin Adeney and John Lloyd, *Miners' Strike, 1984–85: Loss Without Limit* (1985).

Huw Beynon (ed), *Digging Deeper: Issues in the Miners' Strike* (1985).

Idris Davies, *Gwalia Deserta* (1938).

Hywel Francis, *The Tower Story: Lessons in Vigilance and Freedom* (1997).

Hywel Francis, *Magnificent Seven: A Centenary History of Seven Sisters RFC* (1997).

Hywel Francis and David Smith, *The Fed: A History of the South Wales Miners in the Twentieth Century* (reprinted 1998).

Mair Francis, *Up the DOVE! The History of the DOVE Workshop in Banwen* (2008).

Geoffrey Goodman, *The Miners' Strike* (1985).

Christopher Hill, *The Experience of Defeat* (1984).

John Morgans, *Journey of a Lifetime* (2008).

Tyrone O'Sullivan, *Tower of Strength* (2001).

Vickie Seddon (ed), *The Cutting Edge: Women and the Pit Strike* (1985).

Alan Thornett (ed), *The Miners' Strike in Oxford* (1985).

Valleys Initiative for Adult Education, *Chasing the Dragon: Creative Community Responses to the Crisis in the South Wales Coalfield* (1996).

Peter Walker, *Staying Power* (1991).

Raymond Williams, *Resources of Hope* (1989).

ARTICLES AND BOOK CHAPTERS BY HYWEL FRANCIS

'Argraffiadau Cyntaf Streic y Glowyr', *Barn*, Ebrill (1985), pp. 139-144.

'Coalfield Conundrums', *Marxism Today* (Sept 1987), pp. 28-29.

'Denial of Dignity', *New Statesman* (Sept 1989), pp. 10-11.

'Hanging on in The Valleys', *The Valleys Project* (1986), pp. 32-35.

'History Invades the Valleys', *The Valleys Project* (1984), pp. 1-3.

'Mewn Undeb mae Nerth – a Gwersi', *Y Faner*, Gorffenaf 20 (1984), pp. 14-15.

'Mining the Popular Front', *Marxism Today* (Feb 1985), pp. 12-15.

'No Surrender in the Valleys: The 1984–85 Miners' Strike in South Wales', *Llafur* (1989), pp. 41-71 (with Gareth Rees).

'NUM: Fight, Fight and Fight Again', *Marxism Today* (Aug 1987), pp. 22-24.

'NUM United: A Team in Disarray', *Marxism Today* (April 1985), pp. 28-34.

South Wales Echo 20th Anniversary Special (March 2005), p.12.

Striking Back (1985), pp. 5, 10-14, 15-24.
(Penny Smith and Phil Thomas)

The Journal of Law of Society: The State v. The People (1985), pp. 267-271.

'The Valleys' in Richard Jenkins and Arwel Edwards (eds), *One Step Forward? South and West Wales Towards 2000* (1990) pp109 - 118.

'Unfinished Business: The Breaking of the NUM?', *Marxism Today* (Aug 1985), pp. 22-24.

DISSERTATION

Mair Francis, 'Women and the Aftermath of the 1984–85 Miners' Strike: A South Wales Analysis', Swansea University MSc Econ Dissertation (1995).

OTHER ARTICLES/PAMPHLETS

David Howell, 'The 1984–85 Miners' Strike in North Wales' in *Contemporary Wales* vol. 4 (1991).

'Betrayal at Blaengarw' in *Radical Wales* (Spring 1986), p. 4.

Victoria Winckler, *Rethinking Regeneration: The Heads of the Valleys*, Bevan Foundation Platform Series (2008).

About the Author

Hywel Francis has been inextricably linked to the South Wales mining community all his life. He and his wife, Mair, and all their children, Hannah, Dafydd and Sam, were all active participants in campaigning in support of the miners' cause in 1984–85. Towards the end of the strike, Mair was the prime mover in the setting up of DOVE, a women's training workshop at Banwen that grew out of the local women's support group in the Dulais Valley. She is now its president and recently published its history, *Up the DOVE!* (2008).

Hywel Francis was born in the mining community of Onllwyn in the Dulais Valley, the first in five generations (on both sides of the family) not to 'go underground'. His father, Dai Francis, was the general secretary of the South Wales Area of the NUM (1963–76) and the first chair of the Wales TUC (1975).

With Dai Smith, Hywel was the official historian of the miners' union, publishing *The Fed: A History of the South Wales Miners in the Twentieth Century* (1980, reprinted 1998). He also published *Miners Against Fascism: Wales and the Spanish Civil War* (1984, reprinted 2004).

He was the founder in 1973 of the South Wales Miners' Library at Swansea University and an organiser of trade union day release courses for the NUM (1975–90) and community education programmes in the valleys which culminated in the creation of the Valleys Initiative for Adult Education (1987) and the Community University of the Valleys (1993).

During the miners' strike he was chair of both the Neath Dulais and Swansea Valleys Miners' Support Group and the

Wales Congress in Support of Mining Communities and was on the editorial board of *Marxism Today*. He wrote extensively on the strike in such diverse journals as *Barn, Y Faner, Marxism Today, New Socialist* and *The New Statesman*, as well as chapters in *Striking Back* (1985).

He was made a member of the Gorsedd of the National Eisteddfod in Cardigan in 1986 in recognition of his writing and campaigning for the South Wales miners.

He has been Labour MP for Aberavon since 2001. He is currently chair of the Select Committee on Welsh Affairs and a trustee of the Bevan Foundation, the independent social justice think tank.

Before entering Parliament he was Professor of Continuing Education at Swansea University.

Acknowledgements

My first and biggest debt is to my wife Mair who has been a constant source of support in the writing of this book but more importantly was the sole reason that I was able to be so politically active during the miners' strike and for the whole of that turbulent decade. She once told a friend that she only knew where I was going by eavesdropping on my telephone conversations.

Mair held the home together with my late mother Catherine, a stalwart of earlier strikes including 1926. Our three children, Hannah, Dafydd and Sam were also active in their own way – Hannah and Dafydd even went out on picket lines and Sam, joined them on demonstrations. As a family, like so many across Britain whose roots or sympathies were with the miners, we became part of the struggle. Mair participated in the support groups and towards the end of the strike set up a women's co-operative which became known as DOVE.

I want to thank friends in my local miners' support group and the Wales Congress for sharing their memories. In particular I wish to thank Hefina Headon, Christine Powell, Meri Hughes, Simon Jones, Rev John Morgans and Wayne Thomas of the NUM and my parliamentary colleagues Sian James (who also provided me with photographs), Mick Clapham, David Hamilton, Dennis Skinner and Kim Howells, all of whom had prominent roles in the strike.

I am grateful to Sian Williams at the South Wales Miners' Library and Elisabeth Bennett of the South Wales Coalfield

Archive at Swansea University and staff at the House of Commons Library for their assistance.

I wish to thank Martin Shakeshaft for permission to use his photographs and Roger Davies of Swansea University for help with the reproduction of photographs as well as Tim Fearnside of Swansea University for the production of the map of the South Wales coalfield. I trust I have acknowledged all other photographers throughout the book.

Professor Gareth Rees has been especially generous in allowing me to use the article which we jointly wrote that was published in *Llafur* entitled 'No Surrender in the Valleys' (1989), as has Neil Evans, the joint editor of *Llafur*. I thank Martin Jacques (formerly editor of *Marxism Today*) for allowing me to use parts of articles I wrote for *Marxism Today*, Penny Smith and Professor Phil Thomas for parts of chapters I wrote in *Striking Back* (1985) and Richard Jenkins and Arwel Edwards for allowing me to use parts of my chapter 'The Valleys' in their edited collection, *One Step Forward? South and West Wales Towards 2000* (1990).

Tyrone O'Sullivan, a good friend and comrade since 1973, was kind enough to write the foreword and in doing so reminds us what a big part he and Tower have played in recent struggles in the coal industry and indeed in the contemporary history of Wales.

Finally I wish to thank Lucy Llewellyn and Dominic Williams of Iconau for their professionalism, patience and enthusiasm in making this publication possible. Any errors of judgement or accuracy are all my own.

UP THE DOVE tells the important story of the DOVE Workshop – a 'shining beacon' in the Dulais valley.

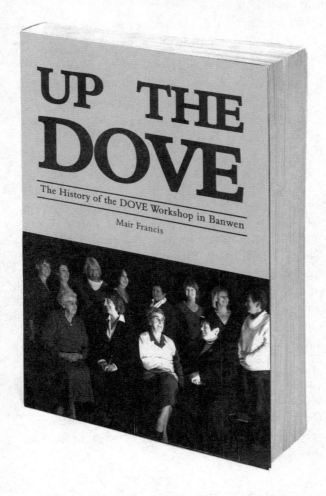

Order your copy online from:

gwales.com
Llyfrau ar-lein
Books on-line

Born during the miners' strike 1984–85, the DOVE Workshop was set up by a group of women with a common purpose that strove to save their communities. This history traces its development as a community education and training resource and effective social enterprise.

£9.99   ISBN: 978-1-905762-72-9